Natural Cleaning: How to Clean Your Home Naturally

by Rachel Jones

This book contains material protected under International and Federal Copyright Laws and Treaties. Any unauthorized reprint or use of this material is prohibited. No part of this book may be reproduced or transmitted in any form or by any means, electronic or mechanical, including photocopying, recording, or by any information storage and retrieval system without express written permission from the author.

© 2013. All rights reserved.

Disclaimer:

This book is for entertainment purposes only. The publisher and author of this book are not responsible for any damages arising directly or indirectly from use of the information in this book. Use this information at your own risk. The publisher and author disclaim any liabilities for damages caused by use of the information contained herein.

None of the claims in this book should be construed as medical advice. Consult with a medical professional prior to making any changes in your life that could impact your health.

Contents

The Benefits of Natural Green Cleaners 9
The Hazards of Chemical Cleansers 12
    Toxic Chemicals Found in Household Cleaning Products 15
        2-Butoxyethanol 16
        Allergens 17
        Ammonia 18
        Carcinogens 19
        Perchloroethylene 20
        Phthalates 21
        Triclosan 22
Greenwashing: Commercial "Green" Cleaners 23
The Transition: Easing In vs. the Big Switch 25
Trial and Error 27
Essential Oils Aren't Just for Scent 29
    Lavender Essential Oil 32
    Lemon Essential Oil 34
    Peppermint Essential Oil 35
    Tea Tree Essential Oil 36
    Eucalyptus Essential Oil 37
Baking Soda and Washing Soda 39
    Using Baking Soda on its Own 41

Washing Soda 44
Baking Soda and Washing Soda Recipes 46
　Carpet Cleaner 47
　Color Catchers 48
　Cutting Board Cleaner 49
　Dish Detergent (Powder) 50
　Fizzy Cleaners 51
　Marble Cleaner 53
　Room Deodorizer 54
　Sticky Residue Remover 55
　Stove Top Cleaner 56
　Toilet Cleaner 57
　Towel Cleaner 58
　Window Screen Cleaner 59
Borax 60
　Borax Safety 61
　Ways to Use Borax 63
　Borax Recipes 65
　　Ant Killer 66
　　Dishwasher Detergent (powder) 67
　　Drain Cleaner 68
　　Flower Preserver 69
　　Rust Remover 70
　　Scouring Paste 71

Sink Stain Remover 72
Castile Soap... 73
   Making Liquid Castile Soap from Bar Soap 74
   Uses for Castile Soap 76
   Castile Soap Recipes 77
      All-Purpose Cleaner 78
      Antibacterial Hand Soap 79
      Dish Soap (Liquid).. 80
      Dishwasher Detergent (Liquid)............................. 81
      Laundry Soap (Powdered)...................................... 83
      Laundry Soap (Liquid)... 84
      Oven Cleaner... 85
      Tub and Tile Cleaner.. 86
      Window Cleaner.. 87
Hydrogen Peroxide... 88
   Uses for Hydrogen Peroxide 90
   Hydrogen Peroxide Recipes 91
      Disinfectant Spray... 92
      Barbecue Grill Cleaner... 93
      Grout Cleaner 94
      Stain Remover 95
      Whitening Toothpaste 96
Salt 97
   Uses for Salt 98

Salt Recipes 99
    Brass and Copper Cleaner 100
    Metal Polish 101
    Rust Removal Paste 102
    Silver Polish 103
    Silver Tarnish Remover 104
    Oven Spill Cleaner 105
    Pot and Pan Cleaner 106
    Wood Polish 107
Vinegar 108
    Uses for Vinegar 109
    Vinegar Recipes 111
        Air Freshener 112
        All-Purpose Cleaner 113
        Carpet Stain Remover 114
        Coffee Maker Cleaner 115
        Foaming Drain Cleaner 116
        Leather Revitalizer 117
        Mineral Deposit Remover 118
        Mold Cleaner 119
        Wood Revitalizer 120
        Wood Scratch Remover 121
Cleaning Specific Areas of the House 122
    Flooring and Carpet 123

- Carpet 124
- Hardwood Floors 126
- Laminate Floors 129
- Linoleum 131
- Marble 132
- Tile Floors 134
- Vinyl Floors 137

Counters 139
- Granite and Marble 141
- Tile 143
- Laminate 144
- Concrete 145
- Wood 147

The Kitchen and Dining Room 149
- The Refrigerator 150
- Cabinets 152
- The Sink and Garbage Disposal 153
- Dishwashing 154
- The Oven and Microwave 156
- Coffee Maker 158
- The Table 159

Bathroom 160
- Mirrors 161
- Shower and Tub 162

- Toilets.. 165
- Deodorizing the Room 167
- Septic Tank... 169
- Living Room... 171
  - Furniture 172
  - Windows and Window Treatments.................... 174
  - TVs and Monitors 177
  - Fireplace 178
- Bedrooms... 180
  - Bedding 181
  - Mattresses.. 182
- Laundry Room... 184
  - Washers and Dryers 185
  - Laundry 186
- Keeping the House Clean.. 189
- Appendix: Recipe Quick Reference Guide 193

The Benefits of Natural Green Cleaners

When you go green with your household cleaning products, you'll begin to reap a number of benefits. Some are immediately noticeable, while others aren't so obvious at first glance. The decisions you make regarding the cleaners you use in your home impact both your health and the health of the environment.

The most important benefits of "going green" are those related to the safety of natural cleaning products in comparison to synthetic cleansers. Natural cleaning products are less toxic and are much safer to use around the house than their harsh and caustic chemical counterparts.

You, your children and even your pets will be much better off living in a home cleaned using non-toxic cleaners. You won't have to worry about children or pets touching, drinking or otherwise coming in contact with highly toxic chemical compounds and you'll be able to sleep better at night knowing you aren't inadvertently poisoning the ones you love every time they come in contact with surfaces you've just cleaned.

Instead of filling your home with indoor pollutants, you'll be filling it with natural compounds and pleasant scents. Your house will be free of the neurotoxins, carcinogens and heavy metals found in commercial cleaners and you'll be happier and healthier as a result.

In addition to protecting your loved ones, you'll be protecting the environment. Instead of polluting the planet with toxic chemical compounds that negatively impact any living creature they come in contact with, you'll be using natural cleaners that are biodegradable and break down into natural elements.

Instead of polluting the planet, you'll be making it a better place.

Another major benefit of switching to natural cleaners is the cost. Some of you are probably shaking your head right now because you've priced natural cleaning products at the store and decided against using them because they cost as much as double the price of the chemical cleansers. Manufacturers know natural cleaning products are hot commodity right now and they've jacked the prices up as a result. The solution to avoiding paying more for natural cleaning products is to make them yourself.

I'm going to show you how to make simple natural cleaning products at home that aren't just cheaper than the green cleaning products sold in stores; they cost a fraction of what you're currently paying for chemical cleansers. Instead of buying specialized cleaners designed to clean specific areas of the house, you'll only be buying a handful of natural items that can be bought in bulk for pennies on the dollar in comparison to synthetic cleaners. You'll then be able to mix these items to make cleaners that can be used to clean pretty much anything in the house.

The best part about going green with your household cleaning is you don't lose any cleaning power in the process. From what I've seen, green cleaners almost always work as well as chemical cleaners, and in some cases, the green cleaners are far superior to the synthetic versions.

You've got everything to lose and nothing to gain by continuing to use chemical cleaners in your home. It's time to make the switch to non-toxic natural cleaners. Ask yourself... Is a clean house really clean if the substances being used to clean it are highly toxic? Or are you simply killing germs and bacteria and replacing them with something that's just as bad for your health?

The Hazards of Chemical Cleansers

When most people purchase commercial household cleaning supplies, they pay little mind to what's actually in the products they're purchasing. Cleaning supplies are purchased based on what the label says they do, ignoring the actual ingredients used to make the cleaner. As long as our counters are spotless and our homes smell good and are germ-free, we don't concern ourselves with minor details like what's actually in the bottle.

Manufacturers know people are far more concerned with what a cleaning product can do *for them* than they are with what it's doing *to them*. This allows unscrupulous companies to use inexpensive chemical compounds that work as advertised, but are highly toxic when touched, inhaled or ingested. Our homes look and smell great, but at what cost?

Here are just some of the risks associated with chemical cleaning products:

- **Skin and eye irritation.** Some of the chemicals used in commercial cleaning products cause irritation upon contact with the skin, eyes and other sensitive areas. Corrosive cleaning products like drain cleaners and oven degreasers contain chemicals that can cause severe burns if they come in direct contact with the skin.
- **Dangerous fumes.** Inhaling the fumes from cleaning products can have potentially dangerous results. The fumes from some harsh chemical

cleaners can burn the mouth, throat, esophagus and lungs. These toxic fumes can also touch off a severe respiratory response when inhaled and the gases created when certain chemicals are mixed can permanently damage the lungs.

- **Chemical fragrances.** That fresh lemon scent probably isn't the result of real lemon being added to the cleaning product. Chemical fragrance blends are added to household cleaning products to make them smell good, but these chemicals are anything but good for you. They can irritate the respiratory system and may touch off an immune system response that causes headaches, nausea and a number of other side effects. Fragrance blends are considered trade secrets, so manufacturers aren't required to list the ingredients of their fragrances on the label. There's no telling what you're being exposed to.
- **Hormone disruption.** Hormone-blocking compounds found in some household cleaning products may increase the possibility of birth defects and up the risk of cancer.
- **Increased risk of cancer.** Long-term exposure to certain chemicals found in popular household cleaning products has been shown to increase the likelihood of developing cancer. Household cleaning products are known to contain carcinogenic compounds that are readily absorbed into the skin. Minimizing exposure to these chemicals may reduce the risk of developing cancer down the road.

In addition to the health hazards associated with chemical cleaning agents, they carry the added bonus of being highly toxic to the environment. They get flushed down the toilet and washed down the drains in large amounts, as tens of millions of people clean their homes daily. The chemicals travel through sewage systems and eventually reach water treatment plants. These plants are tasked with cleaning the sewage and chemical-laden water and do a pretty good job of it, but some of the chemical compounds remain in the water once cleaning is complete.

Once the water is processed by the treatment plant, it's discharged into our lakes, rivers and waterways. The chemical compounds left in the water can wreak havoc on the environment. They disrupt reproductive systems in fish and wildlife and are responsible for a number of birth defects. The phosphates in some detergents can touch off algae blooms that deplete lakes and reservoirs of oxygen, killing fish and other aquatic creatures.

A house cleaned with synthetic cleaners is full of a compendium of toxic chemicals, harsh fumes and dangerous substances. These substances can impact both the health of the people in the house and the health of the environment into which the cleaners are discharged.

Luckily, there's a safe alternative to chemical cleaners. Natural household cleaning products provide an avenue through which you can safely and effectively clean your house without having to turn to toxic and expensive synthetic products.

Toxic Chemicals Found in Household Cleaning Products

It's all but impossible to completely avoid exposure to toxic chemicals, but there's no reason to needlessly expose ourselves to them day in and day out. The chemicals in this chapter are commonly found in household cleaners and should be avoided at all costs.

If you aren't well-versed as to what's in the cleaning products you've been using, the information you're about to learn will come as a surprise. I know I was shocked when I realized exactly what was in the products I'd been using to "clean" my home. The chemical compounds found in household cleaners can be highly toxic and potentially deadly. In the case of commercial cleaners, what you don't know really can hurt you.

Keep in mind this section isn't all-inclusive. It's designed to give you an idea of some of the worst toxins found in chemical cleaners. There are numerous other compounds in commercial cleaners that are bad news. These are just some of the most prevalent and well-known hazardous compounds.

2-Butoxyethanol

2-butoxyethanol is categorized as a glycol ether, which places it in a class of dangerous solvents that are heavily regulated in the workplace, but for some reason it's allowed in window, glass and household cleaners. It can be absorbed through the skin, by ingesting it or the particles can be inhaled as they float through the air. 2-butoxyethanol goes by a number of names, including 2-BE and butyl cellosolve.

When inhaled in large amounts, this powerful solvent can cause pulmonary edema and can severely damage the liver and kidneys. In small amounts, it can cause headaches, nausea, narcosis, coughing and shortness of breath. Exposure to large amounts can result in blood disorders. Using cleaning products containing 2-BE in an enclosed area can cause the amount of 2-BE in the air to rapidly build up to dangerous levels.

Oddly enough, 2-butoxyethanol is found in some "green" cleaning products. Manufacturers that add it to their products probably do so because it isn't considered harmful to the environment since it biodegrades rapidly.

Allergens

Allergens encompass a broad range of chemical compounds found in cleaning products. The most common allergens are found in the synthetic fragrance blends added to commercial cleaners. Different people are allergic to different compounds, so there's no telling what compound might cause an allergic reaction.

Exposure to allergens can cause symptoms ranging from mild symptoms like watering eyes, rashes, and coughing to more severe symptoms like migraine headaches, chronic dermatitis and asthma. If you're experiencing the symptoms of an allergic reaction, but can't pin down where it's coming from, it may be due to allergens found in cleaning products used in the home.

Labeling requirements for potential allergens are lax in the United States. The European Union has stricter standards regarding allergens in home cleaning products and requires manufacturers to label products that contain certain allergens. The labels are changed to eliminate the allergen warnings in the United States. Thanks a lot, manufacturers.

Ammonia

Because it cleans without causing streaks, ammonia is used in a number of cleaning products used to clean shiny surfaces. Bathroom fixtures, sinks, jewelry and glass cleaners are a small sampling of products that commonly contain ammonia.

Ammonia causes a strong respiratory reaction when inhaled, which can be compounded in people who have asthma or other respiratory problems. Prolonged repeated exposure to ammonia can lead to long-term respiratory issues like chronic bronchitis and asthma. Mixing products containing ammonia with products containing bleach creates a toxic cloud of chloramine gas. Inhalation of this gas can result in loss of consciousness and even death.

Some green products contain ammonia and it isn't unheard of to find green recipes that call for it. I've intentionally avoided ammonia in this book because of its potential to cause health problems in some individuals.

Carcinogens

Carcinogens are compounds known to cause cancer. **Suspected carcinogens** are compounds thought to cause cancer. There are a number of known and suspected carcinogens found in household cleaning products.

The following compounds found in cleaning products are possibly linked to increased risk of cancer in people exposed to them:

- **1,4-Dichlorobenzene.**
- **Acid blue 9.**
- **Alkylphenols.**
- **Aluminum silicate.**
- **Crystalline silica.**
- **Diathanolamine (DEA).**
- **Formaldehyde.**
- **Morpholine.**
- **Ortho phenylphenol.**
- **Petroleum byproducts.**
- **Petroleum hydrocarbons.**
- **Sodium ortho-phenylphenol.**
- **Tetrachloretheylene.**
- **Triclosan.**
- **Triethanolamine.**

Keep in mind this is just a small sampling of the possible carcinogens found in household cleaning products. There are a number of chemical compounds not on the list that are potentially unsafe.

Perchloroethylene

Perchloroethylene (PERC) is commonly found in degreasers, solvents, wood cleaners, spot removers and carpet and upholstery cleaners. It goes by a number of names, including the following:

- **Perchloroethylene.**
- **PERC.**
- **Tetrachloroethylene.**
- **Tetrachlorethylene.**
- **PCE.**

Short-term exposure to PERC can cause nausea and headaches, while long-term exposure opens you up to damage to the respiratory system, liver, kidneys and central nervous system. To top things off, it's listed as a carcinogen by the National Toxicology Program and long-term exposure has been linked to a number of cancers.

Phthalates

Phthalates are a family of chemicals that are commonly used to make plastic and vinyl more flexible. They're used in hundreds of products found in the home and are commonly found in scented household cleaning products, where they're added as a carrier to help disperse the fragrance.

The following dangers are thought to be associated with phthalates:

- **Allergies.**
- **Altered behavior.**
- **Birth defects.**
- **Hormone disruption.**
- **Increased cancer risk.**
- **Interference with testosterone production.**
- **Irreversible damage to the development of the male reproductive system.**
- **Obesity .**
- **Reduced fertility.**
- **Worsening of asthma.**

Phthalates can be readily absorbed into the skin, ingested when they come in contact with food items or they can be inhaled and absorbed through the lungs. There's no telling when you're being exposed to phthalates because there are currently no labeling requirements when it comes to products containing them.

Triclosan

Triclosan is used in products like hand soap and dishwashing detergents because of its strong antibacterial qualities.

It works as advertised, killing most bacteria on contact. The key word in the previous sentence is *most*. The bacteria that do survive sometimes mutate and become stronger. Use of triclosan and its close cousin triclocarban create superstrains of bacteria that are resistant to antibiotics. This doesn't just impact your ability to clean the house; it can result in illnesses and bacterial infections that are difficult to treat.

Studies have found triclosan eventually makes its way into our waterways, where it kills off algae. This can negatively impact the health of the entire ecosystem, as the fish and other organisms that feed on the algae run out of food.

Greenwashing: Commercial "Green" Cleaners

Greenwashing is a term used to describe the practice of selling products that are marketed as being green, but contain chemical compounds that are anything but healthy. The public thinks they're getting green products, but the reality is they're purchasing products that are only marginally better than their synthetic counterparts, if at all. The products cost significantly more money, but the net effect of making the switch to these products is minimal, at best.

Walk through the household cleaning section of your local department store and you'll see all sorts of products labeled as non-toxic, biodegradable and green. The labels often feature pictures of nature and the packaging is colored green in an attempt to fool consumers into believing they're getting products that are better for them and are good for the environment. The reality is many of these products contain chemicals like triclosan, 2-butoxyethanol and petro-derived compounds.

The kicker? Since there are no labeling requirements for household products, these chemicals may not be included on the ingredient list. People are being fooled into thinking they're using green alternative cleaners, but all they're really being fooled into doing is spending more money.

The only way to be sure of what's in your green cleaners is to make them yourself at home. You can control exactly what goes into your cleaners, so you'll know they're really green. You'll also save money. A lot of it.

The Transition: Easing In vs. the Big Switch

There are two ways you can make the switch to natural cleaning products. There is no right or wrong choice and there are benefits and pitfalls associated with each of the methods.

I call the first transitioning technique "*Easing In.*" This method allows you to ease in to using green cleaners and is the better choice for those who don't like sudden and drastic change. To ease in, you continue using your chemical cleaners and slowly but surely replace them with natural alternatives as you use them up. It can take quite some time to completely make the switch to green cleaning using this method, but you'll eventually get there. Easing in allows you to avoid suddenly changing your routine and will give you time to adjust to using natural cleaners one at a time.

One big problem associated with easing in is people tend to stock up on household cleaners when they're on sale and often have entire cabinets and shelves full of cleaners. It can take years to use up all of the cleaning products on the shelf—years during which you continue to expose yourself and your family to harsh chemicals and fumes.

The easing in process can be as long or as short as you want it to be. You can wait until you've used up all of your household cleaning products to make the switch or you can slowly phase out synthetic products as you see fit. This allows you to stay in your comfort zone while still moving forward and making good progress toward your ultimate goal of going completely green. You can start small and work your way forward a step or two at a time. Once you start getting comfortable making your own products, you can accelerate the transition.

The second transitioning technique is more of an all-or-nothing approach. The "*Big Switch*" requires that you toss out all of your household cleaning products and switch over to natural products immediately. This approach is the healthier approach because it immediately eliminates all chemical cleaning products from the home. The problem with this method is it's such a drastic change people tend to panic and want to go back to their comfort zone.

What I recommend is doing whatever you're comfortable with. If you don't like change, easing into green cleaning would likely be the better choice. On the other hand, if the thought of continuing to use chemical cleaners disgusts you and you think you can handle it, making an immediate switch would be the better option.

No matter what you decide, do something. No matter what you do, you'll be moving forward with creating a better environment both inside and outside your home. That's what really matters.

Trial and Error

The recipes contained in this book aren't set in stone. They're solid recipes that have been proven to work on a number of surfaces, but they may not be the perfect blend of ingredients to suit your personal needs. One of the perks of making your own cleaning products is you can adjust the ingredients to suit your needs. If you find certain ingredients work better than others, you can make your own recipes that incorporate those ingredients.

Certain products work better on some surfaces than they do on others. You never know exactly how a surface is going to react to a cleaning product until you've actually tested the recipe on the surface. While most of the natural ingredients used in the recipes in this book are fairly benign, they may not produce the desired results when used on certain surfaces. It's always a good idea to test your cleaning products on a small area first to see if anything unexpected happens.

Don't be afraid to experiment. Some of my best recipes have come about as a result of me wondering what would happen if I tried something new. Green cleaning is all about figuring out the natural products that work best for the surfaces in your home. There's no one-size-fits-all solution that works for everyone.

It's best to start small and try the simple recipes first. You'll be amazed at how many surfaces you'll be able to clean with hydrogen peroxide or vinegar alone. There's no reason to make complex recipes for items you can clean using a single natural product.

    If a single product doesn't work, it's time to start trying recipes. Keep a pen and pad of paper handy when you're getting started. You might think you'll remember which recipes and products work on certain surfaces in your house while they're fresh in your mind, but you'll be racking your brain trying to remember all of them months down the road.

Essential Oils Aren't Just for Scent

A number of the recipes in this book call for essential oils. For those not already familiar with **essential oils**, they're concentrated versions of the volatile oils that give plants their signature smell. Essential oils are extracted from the plant using a number of methods, ranging from steam distillation to solvent extraction. The cost of the oil is usually directly related to the distillation method used to obtain the oil and how difficult it is to obtain.

Some plants yield large amounts of oil per plant, while others yield only a minute amount.

Most essential oils smell like the plant they're derived from. Lemon essential oil smells strongly of lemon, eucalyptus essential oil has the strong scent of eucalyptus and lavender oil smells like concentrated lavender flowers. Other oils like tea tree oil have unique scents that take a bit of getting used to.

There are a number of health benefits thought to be associated with essential oils. The mere scent of these concentrated plant oils is said to carry a number of health benefits. Adding essential oils to your recipes makes them smell good and may make you healthier as a result.

Getting started in the world of essential oils can be confusing because there are various grades of essential oils sold by different manufacturers. Therapeutic grade, certified grade, aromatherapy grade and medicinal grade oils are all sold on the open market. These terms are meaningless in the grand scheme of things because there are no standards to which essential oils are held. The exact same term could be used by two different companies and their oils could be of vastly different quality.

While the quality of essential oils used for household cleaning products isn't as important as that of essential oils used for aromatherapy and topical application, it's still important you seek out pure oils that are unaltered and unadulterated. Adulteration is a process through which more expensive oils are diluted with cheaper additives to make them less costly. While some suppliers label adulterated oils, others have been known to adulterate oils without notifying customers.

Avoid oils that are solvent-extracted because the manufacturers use harsh solvents that are decidedly not environmentally friendly. Trace amounts of these solvents make it into the final product.

It's important to buy essential oils from established companies that have a good reputation in the aromatherapy industry. The following companies are generally believed to be good companies to purchase essential oils from:

- Aura Cacia - http://www.auracacia.com
- Floracopeia - http://www.floracopeia.com
- Mountain Rose Herbs - http://www.mountainroseherbs.com/
- Veriditas Botanicals - http://veriditasbotanicals.com/

A lot of people I know swear by the Young Living and doTerra brands of essential oils, but I've never tried them. I do know they cost quite a bit, but I rarely hear a bad review of these oils. Be aware both companies are run as multi-level marketing companies and may try to sign you up as a supplier.

What I've found is there is no single supplier that makes great essential oils across the board. Quality varies from oil to oil and sometimes even from batch to batch. Find a supplier or set of suppliers you're happy with and constantly be on the lookout for changes in quality of the oil.

The rest of the chapter discusses a handful of the most popular oils amongst natural cleaning enthusiasts. Keep in mind there are hundreds of oils to choose from and this is just a small sampling of what's available. When you consider essential oils can be mixed and matched to create oil blends, you have thousands or even tens of thousands of choices when it comes to scents for your products.

Lavender Essential Oil

Lavender oil is made from the lavender plant. Lavender essential oil is one of the most popular and versatile essential oils in the world, and for good reason. It has a fresh floral scent that somehow manages to be both relaxing and invigorating at the same time.

Lavender oil is believed to have the following properties:

- **Antibacterial.**
- **Anti-inflammatory.**
- **Antiseptic.**
- **Antiviral.**
- **Calming.**
- **Deodorant.**
- **Sedative.**

This sweet-scented oil doesn't just smell good. It has deodorant properties that eliminate bad smells at the source. Mildew, sweat, tobacco smoke, etc.. You name it; lavender oil will make short work of it.

One of the downsides of cleaning with vinegar is the acrid smell vinegar lets loose when you spray it in a room. The smell is short-lived, but if you're anything like me, you don't care for the burning nostrils and watery eyes that accompany the strong smell of vinegar. Adding lavender oil to homemade products containing vinegar knocks down the odor of the vinegar, leaving rooms it's used in smelling like flowers.

Add lavender oil to products you want to use on surfaces that need to be disinfected. The antibacterial and antiseptic qualities of lavender oil will help eliminate harmful microorganisms.

This is one oil you don't want to pass on. It'll be the most versatile oil in your arsenal.

Lemon Essential Oil

Everyone loves the smell of lemon scented housecleaning products and **lemon essential oil** is one of the best ways to add natural lemon scent to your recipes. 5 to 10 drops are all it takes to add lemon scent to most recipes.

Lemon essential oil is believed to have the following properties:

- **Antimicrobial.**
- **Antiseptic.**
- **Antibacterial.**
- **Purifying.**
- **Insecticidal.**
- **Tonic.**

If you've got a tough cleaning job on your hands, adding lemon essential oil to the cleaning product you're using will help you make short work of grease, sap and other difficult to clean substances. In addition to cutting through grease and grime, lemon essential oil disinfects and deodorizes, leaving your house and your clothes clean and smelling fresh.

Peppermint Essential Oil

Be careful when using **peppermint essential oil**. It's generally considered safe in small amounts, but does contain menthol and other compounds that can irritate the skin, eyes and lungs when used improperly. A few drops of peppermint oil are usually all that's needed in your house cleaning products.

Peppermint essential oil has the following properties:

- **Anesthetic.**
- **Antibacterial.**
- **Antifungal.**
- **Antiseptic.**
- **Astringent.**
- **Decongestant.**
- **Stimulant.**

Peppermint oil adds a refreshing, minty scent to recipes it's added to. The scent is invigorating and can help you make it through long cleaning sessions. While you might love the scent of peppermint, household pests hate it and it can be used to keep insects, rodents and other small critters at bay.

Tea Tree Essential Oil

Tea tree essential oil comes from the leaves of the Melaleuca tree, which is a tree that's native to Australia. It has a spicy, camphorous scent that takes some getting used to. Most people don't care for the smell of tea tree oil the first time they smell it, but it grows on you after a while. If you really don't care for the smell on its own, it can be combined with lemon or lavender oil to create a blended smell that's more familiar.

The following therapeutic properties have been associated with tea tree essential oil:

- **Antimicrobial.**
- **Antiseptic.**
- **Antifungal.**
- **Antiviral.**
- **Antibacterial.**
- **Insecticide.**
- **Stimulant.**

Tea tree essential oil is said to stimulate the immune system and can help clear up congestion and coughs. It has strong antimicrobial properties, making it one of the better essential oils to add to disinfectant cleaning recipes. This oil is also a good choice for recipes used to clean up and prevent mold because it is antifungal.

Eucalyptus Essential Oil

I saved eucalyptus essential oil for last because it's the strongest oil in the group. There are a few precautions that need to be taken when using products containing eucalyptus oil:

- **Keep it out of the reach of children and animals.** Contact poison control immediately if swallowed. Don't use concentrated amounts in areas of the house where kids and animals might come in contact with it.
- **Steer clear of eucalyptus oil when pregnant.** It's believed it may cause uterine contractions.
- **Avoid contact with the eyes, skin and mucous membranes.**
- **Eucalyptus oil may trigger seizures in sensitive individuals.** Do not use this oil if this is of concern.

If you've ever stood in a eucalyptus grove and inhaled deeply, you know what this oil smells like. It's aroma is minty and campherous, so much so it almost burns the nostrils when you breathe deeply of it. It's refreshing and invigorating and will leave your house smelling clean and disinfected. When added to cleaning recipes, its aroma is reminiscent of Lysol.

Eucalyptus essential oil has the following properties:

- **Antibacterial.**
- **Anti-inflammatory.**
- **Antiseptic.**
- **Antiviral.**

- **Astringent.**
- **Decongestant.**
- **Deodorant.**
- **Stimulant.**

Add it to your cleaning products when you have major cleaning and/or deodorizing jobs. It works well on most hard surfaces, but can damage some materials. Always test products containing eucalyptus oil on a small area before using them on an entire surface.

Baking Soda and Washing Soda

Baking soda is known by many different names:

- **Baking soda.**
- **Bicarb soda.**
- **Bicarb.**
- **Bicarbonate of soda.**
- **Bread soda.**
- **Cooking soda.**
- **Saleratus.**
- **Sodium bicarb.**
- **Sodium bicarbonate.**
- **Sodium hydrogen carbonate.**

It exists naturally as a solid white crystalline material and can be created in a laboratory setting through a process called the **Solvay process**, which creates soda ash out of salt brine and limestone. The soda ash is then processed into baking soda.

Most people have at least one box of baking soda in their pantries or refrigerator, as its primary use in the Western world is as a leavening agent in breads and other baked goods. When combined with acids like lemon juice or vinegar, it causes dough or batter to expand, creating the airy texture people desire in breads and other baked goods. Baking soda creates carbon dioxide when it's heated. This reaction causes breads, cakes and other baked goods to rise as they're cooking.

Most people don't realize baking soda has a number of applications outside of the kitchen. It can be used for cleaning and deodorizing and even has personal hygiene applications. Best of all, it's non-toxic and inexpensive. Once you learn how to use baking soda as a natural cleaner, you'll be left wondering how you ever lived without it.

Using Baking Soda on its Own

It's common knowledge that an open box of baking soda can be kept in the fridge to keep odors at bay. It can also be used anywhere else you have odors you'd like to get rid of. Sprinkle it on carpets or on the floor of your garage, place a box in rooms that smell like cigarette smoke or place a box in the bathroom to quickly get rid of nasty smells. Baking soda is an effective deodorant no matter where you use it.

Before we get into recipes that use baking soda, let's look at the many ways baking soda alone can be used:

- **Clean and deodorize ash trays.** Got a smoker in the house? Sprinkle baking soda in the bottom of ash trays to keep them from stinking up the house.
- **Clean and deodorize your carpet by sprinkling baking soda on it prior to vacuuming.**
- **Clean your counters.** Sprinkle baking soda on your countertops and wipe them down with a damp sponge.
- **Combine baking soda and water to make a paste and apply the paste to splinters to help pull them out of the skin.** Wait ten minutes and the splinter should be easy to remove.
- **Dissolve a couple tablespoons of baking soda into two cups of water and use it to gently and safely clean toys.**

- **If you have a septic system, pour a cup or two of baking soda down one of the drains in your house to help balance the pH.**
- **Make a paste by adding 5 tablespoons of water to a cup of baking soda and use it to clean your stove burners, barbecue grill and corroded battery terminals.**
- **Mix a cup of baking soda into a gallon of water and use it to mop the floor.**
- **Pour a box of baking soda down your drain to deodorize it.** Follow it up with boiling water to break loose partial clogs.
- **Soak your dentures in a solution made by adding a couple tablespoons of baking soda to a cup of water.**
- **Sprinkle baking soda into your trash cans to deodorize them.**
- **Sprinkle baking soda on fresh fruit and veggies and rinse them off to get rid of any dirt.**
- **Sprinkle baking soda on your pets to keep them smelling fresh and clean.** No, you shouldn't do this instead of washing them.
- **Use it on stuffed animals and blankets.** Does your kid have a favorite stuffed animal or blanket that's starting to get musty? Sprinkle baking soda on it and let it sit for 30 minutes before brushing or shaking it off.
- **Use it to clean the microwave.** Dissolve ½ a cup of baking soda in a microwave safe bowl filled with warm water. Microwave the contents

of the bowl. This will soften up baked-on grime in the microwave and make it easier to clean.

Baking soda is an abrasive cleaner that can be used in place of scouring cleaners like Comet. It can be used on most surfaces, but always test it in a small area first. It may leave fine scratches on soft surfaces.

Washing Soda

Spend enough time perusing natural cleaning recipes and you'll eventually come across a recipe calling for **washing soda**. Washing soda, also known as **soda ash** or **sodium carbonate**, is a beneficial item to have around the house because it can be used in place of baking soda when extra cleaning power is needed.

Washing soda can be a bit difficult to obtain, especially if you live in rural areas. The good news is it can easily be made from baking soda, which can be found pretty much anywhere there's a grocery store or market. Washing soda is created by heating up baking soda until it breaks down into soda ash, water and carbon dioxide. The water evaporates and the carbon dioxide dissipates into the air, leaving washing soda behind.

Follow these instructions to make your own washing soda from baking soda:

1. **Procure a baking dish or tray.**
2. **Spread a layer of baking soda out across the tray.**
3. **Heat the oven to 400° F.**
4. **Place the baking dish in the oven and heat the baking soda until it turns into washing soda.** Stir it frequently to accelerate the process.

You'll be able to tell when baking soda turns into washing soda because it will look grainier and will become dull in color.

Washing soda is stronger than baking soda. Be careful and always wear gloves when working with recipes that call for washing soda. It's strongly alkaline and can cause skin and eye irritation. Always test washing soda on a small area prior to applying it to larger surfaces.

Baking Soda and Washing Soda Recipes

Baking soda is a powerful cleaner and a deodorant, but you'll occasionally run into cleaning tasks where baking soda alone isn't enough. That's where these recipes come into play. Washing soda can be used when baking soda just doesn't cut it, but be careful. The strength of washing soda makes it more likely to damage sensitive surfaces.

Combining baking soda and vinegar will create a frothy cleaner that has to be used quickly to remain effective. This combination has to be used while it's still foaming. Storing recipes that combine these two powerful cleaning agents will render the recipe ineffective. Create recipes that combine baking soda and vinegar as you need them in order to avoid storing them and rendering them useless.

Carpet Cleaner

White vinegar and baking soda combine to make an effective carpet cleaner that can be used to remove spots and stubborn stains. This combination will foam up and pull most stains to the surface of the carpet, where they can be blotted or vacuumed up.

INGREDIENTS:

½ cup baking soda.

1 cup white vinegar.

DIRECTIONS:

Create a paste by mixing the baking soda and white vinegar together. Scrub the paste into the stained area of the carpet. Let the paste dry and vacuum it up. Repeat this process until the stain is gone.

Color Catchers

Every time you wash a load of colored clothes, some of the dye used on the clothes makes its way into the water in the washing machine. When dark clothes are washed with lighter colored clothes, the dyes float around the machine and can be picked up by lighter colored clothes, changing or dulling their color over time. Color catchers can be tossed in with a load of laundry to pick up some of the dye floating around in the water.

INGREDIENTS:

3 tablespoons washing soda.

2 cups warm water.

Cotton fabric.

DIRECTIONS:

Combine the washing soda and warm water and stir until the washing soda dissolves into the water. Dip the cotton fabric into the solution and let it dry. Cut it into dryer-sheet sized squares and hang the fabric to dry. Toss a sheet in the washing machine with your laundry.

Cutting Board Cleaner

All sorts of nasty bacteria and microorganisms can build up on cutting boards, especially if you use cutting boards made of porous materials like wood. This cleaner can also be used to clean countertops and other flat surfaces in the home, but shouldn't be used on marble or other materials that are sensitive to acid.

INGREDIENTS:

½ cup baking soda.

1 lemon.

DIRECTIONS:

Cut the lemon in half and dip the cut side of the lemon in baking soda. Use the lemon to scrub the baking soda into the cutting board. Let it sit for 10 minutes and wipe the cutting board clean with a damp sponge.

Dish Detergent (Powder)

Commercial dish detergents can leave a soapy film on your dishes. This dish detergent leaves your dishes shiny and clean—and free of spots. It will clump up if there's a lot of moisture in the air, so it's best to make small amounts and to not attempt to store this recipe for long periods of time.

INGREDIENTS:

½ cup citric acid.

½ cup washing soda.

¼ cup baking soda.

5 tablespoons sea salt.

DIRECTIONS:

Combine all of the ingredients and stir them together. Add 1 to 2 tablespoons of this detergent to each load of dishes.

Fizzy Cleaners

Fizzy cleaners bubble and fizz when they're added to water. The citric acid and baking soda start to bubble as soon as they hit the water.

These cleaners can be used to clean toilets and can be used in sinks and tubs that have been filled with water. You can also fill a bucket with water and place an item you want to clean in the bucket. Add the fizzy cleaner to the bucket and scrub it while the cleaner fizzes and bubbles.

INGREDIENTS:

1 ½ cups baking soda.

½ cup citric acid.

20 drops lemon essential oil.

15 drops peppermint essential oil.

Water.

DIRECTIONS:

Combine the citric acid and baking soda and stir them together. Add the essential oils a drop or two at a time and stir them in. Don't add them too fast or you'll cause the baking soda and citric acid to start fizzing. If the mixture isn't damp enough to mold into shape after stirring in the essential oils, add water to a spray bottle and set the bottle to spray a fine mist. Spray the mist on the mixture one spray at a time and work it in until the mixture is damp enough to mold into shapes.

Place the mixture in silicon trays (or an ice cube tray) and pack it in tight. Let it sit for 8 hours before removing the fizzy cleaners from the tray. If done right, they should hold their shape. When you want to use one, toss it in water and wait for it to start fizzing. Once it starts fizzing, start cleaning the item you want to clean.

Marble Cleaner

If you have marble in your home, you've probably marveled at the cost of marble cleaner. A bottle of good marble cleaner can set you back a pretty penny. Fret no more . . . This marble cleaner only requires two ingredients and is every bit as effective at cleaning marble as most commercial cleaners are.

Don't use acids like vinegar or lemon on marble. Acid can etch marble, causing irreversible damage.

INGREDIENTS:

½ cup baking soda.

½ cup water.

DIRECTIONS:

Dampen a cloth and rub the baking soda into the marble with it. Rinse the baking soda off of the marble using water and dry with a soft cloth or towel.

Room Deodorizer

Certain smells like tobacco smoke and sweaty gym clothes tend to linger around a room no matter what you do. Commercial deodorizers mask the smells, but fail to eliminate them, so they eventually come back. This deodorizer actually eliminates the smell, so there's no worry of the smell returning later on down the road.

INGREDIENTS:

½ cup baking soda.

½ cup fresh lemon juice.

DIRECTIONS:

Combine the baking soda and lemon juice in a small bowl and stir it together. Place the bowl in the room with the odor you want to eliminate. Leave it in there until the smell is gone.

Sticky Residue Remover

Sticky residues can be a bear to clean. No matter how long you scrub certain sticky residues and glues, it's almost impossible to make any headway. All you accomplish is moving the residue from one area of the surface to another. This recipe creates a sticky residue remover that's the all-natural equivalent of Goo Gone, the gold standard in commercial glue removers.

This product is mildly abrasive and contains oil, so test it on a small area first.

INGREDIENTS:

1 cup coconut oil.

1 cup baking soda.

5 drops lemon essential oil.

DIRECTIONS:

Gently heat the coconut oil until it turns liquid. Stir in the baking soda and lemon essential oil. Rub the residue remover into the sticky residue you're attempting to remove. Let it sit for 10 minutes and wipe the residue away. Repeat until the residue is gone.

Stove Top Cleaner

If you're like most people, you wait until your stovetop is a greasy mess to clean it. This recipe can be used to make cleaning that dirty stovetop a breeze without having to resort to using harsh chemicals.

INGREDIENTS:

1 cup washing soda.

¼ cup salt.

1 cup hot water.

DIRECTIONS:

Combine the washing soda and salt in bowl and blend together. Sprinkle the mixture generously over the stovetop. Place the water in a spray bottle and heat it up. Spray the hot water over the washing soda/salt on the stovetop. Spray enough to dissolve the salt and washing soda but be careful not to get it so wet it begins to puddle in low spots of the stove. Ideally, you want it to dissolve, but stay where it's at.

Let the mixture sit for 45 minutes before scrubbing the stovetop with a cloth or damp sponge.

Toilet Cleaner

Baking soda followed up with white vinegar will clean and deodorize your toilet. This cleaner can be used and flushed down the toilet immediately or it can be used and left to sit for a while to allow it to really work its way into the dirt and grime in the toilet.

INGREDIENTS:

½ cup baking soda.

1 cup white vinegar.

OPTIONAL: ½ cup hydrogen peroxide.

DIRECTIONS:

Sprinkle the area you're planning on cleaning with baking soda. Spray white vinegar onto the baking soda and watch as it foams up. Use a toilet brush to scrub the toilet. You can flush the toilet right away or leave the solution in the toilet for a while to let it work on stubborn stains. For tough cleaning jobs, flush the solution down the toilet and then wipe it down with hydrogen peroxide.

Towel Cleaner

Towels eventually lose their ability to absorb water and start to smell a bit ripe when you use them. This is because they build up a residue of grease, grime, fabric softener and detergent that combine to prevent them from working effectively. This residue doesn't come out when towels are washed with normal detergent—it gets worse!

Use this two-part treatment to clean the residue from your towels and return them to almost-new condition.

INGREDIENTS:

¾ cup baking soda.

1 cup white vinegar.

DIRECTIONS:

Run a hot water load of towels through your washer with a cup of white vinegar added. Follow this up by running the same load through with hot water and ¾ cup of baking soda added.

Window Screen Cleaner

Spray this cleaner on your window screens and you won't just have clean screens, you'll have the smell of tea tree essential oil being blown into your house every time you have the window open. You can clean your screens and fill your house with pleasant scents at the same time.

INGREDIENTS:

¼ cup baking soda.

4 cups water.

5 drops tea tree essential oil.

DIRECTIONS:

Combine the water, baking soda and tea tree essential oil in a spray bottle and blend them together. To use the screen cleaner, mist it directly onto the window screens and wipe them down with a soft cloth.

Borax

Borax, also known as **sodium tetraborate** or **sodium borate**, is a natural substance that's mined from the ground. When seasonal lakes fill up and then dry out over the course of many years, deposits of this powerful compound are left behind. There are large deposits of borax in California and smaller deposits in the Southwestern United States.

When borax is mined from the ground, it's in crystalline form. The crystals are pulverized into powder form, which is the form in which borax is commonly sold in stores. One of the most common brands of borax is the 20-Mule Team brand, which is named after the teams of mules originally used to haul the borax to the trains that shipped it out of the desert.

Borax Safety

There's a lot of confusion as to the safety of borax. Look up borax as a cleaning product on the Internet and you'll find a deluge of comments regarding the safety of borax on sites that recommend it as a natural cleaning product.

Borax is one of the more potent all-natural cleaners.

It's a strongly alkaline substance and it can cause skin and respiratory tract irritation if it comes in contact with the skin or is inhaled. Ingesting borax can cause nausea, vomiting, diarrhea and a number of other side effects. It's toxic in extremely high amounts, but isn't a whole lot more dangerous than salt or baking soda. European products containing borax have to be labeled "may damage fertility" or "may damage the unborn child," so it's probably a good idea to avoid products containing borax while pregnant.

According to the Material Safety Data Sheet for borax, it isn't any more toxic than table salt. Many of the studies done on borax are actually done using boric acid, which is created when borax reacts to an acid. Boric acid is highly acidic instead of alkaline, which probably means it has a vastly different effect on the body.

If you do decide to incorporate borax into your household cleaning regimen, a few necessary precautions should be taken. Wear gloves, eye protection and a mask when cleaning with products containing borax and keep it out of the reach of animals and children.

It's up to the individual to determine whether borax is appropriate for use in their home. It appears to be relatively safe in the diluted amounts used in natural household cleaning products, but can be dangerous in higher concentrations. As with all household cleaning products, exercise caution when using items containing borax.

Ways to Use Borax

It's up to the individual to determine whether Borax is a good fit for their natural cleaning needs. It does have its benefits, as evidenced by its many household uses. Borax disinfects and deodorizes as it cleans, making it a strong and effective household cleaning product both in natural cleaning recipes and on its own.

Here are some of the many ways borax can be used around the house:

- **It can be used to kill mold, mildew and fungus.**
- **It is strongly antibacterial, so it can be used as a disinfectant cleaner.**
- **Add it to laundry to soften hard water and to help clean clothes.**
- **Use borax and a wet sponge to remove soap scum and water stains from the shower walls and the bathtub.**
- **Borax can be used as an herbicide.** Sprinkle it anywhere you don't want weeds to grow. Be aware it'll kill any plants it comes in contact with, so don't use it anywhere you want to grow plants.
- **Sprinkle borax in the bottom of your garbage can to keep insects at bay and minimize odors.**
- **Sprinkle borax around openings to the house to keep mice out.**

- **Clean dirty pots and pans with borax and warm water.** It's a non-abrasive cleaner that will cut through grease and grime.
- **Skip the stain stick and rub a paste made by mixing 1 part borax with 2 parts water into stained clothing.** Let it sit for 15 to 20 minutes and then put it through the laundry.
- **Combine a tablespoon of borax with a cup of hot water to make an all-purpose cleaner that's safe on most surfaces.**
- **Add a cup of borax to your toilet and let it sit for a half hour.** Use a toilet brush to scrub the toilet.

Borax Recipes

The recipes in this section combine the natural cleaning powers of borax with other natural cleaners and fragrances to create powerful all-natural household cleaning products. Grab a pair of gloves and get to work. The house isn't going to clean itself!

Ant Killer

I can attest to the fact this recipe kills ants. I have friends who swear it kills roaches as well. I haven't had the opportunity to try it on roaches myself and I hope I never have to. I can't attest to whether it's effective on other insects, but it might be worth a shot.

INGREDIENTS:

1 cup borax.

1 cup granulated sugar.

DIRECTIONS:

Sprinkle the sugar and borax evenly across the area where you're seeing the ants. Your ant problem should clear up quickly. Alternatively, combine the sugar and borax and sprinkle it all the way around the perimeter of the house. This should keep ants out of the house for a week or two.

Try stirring this bug killer into a quart of hot water. The resultant liquid can be placed in a spray bottle and used to spray infested areas. It can also be placed in a container and set out as an ant trap that'll clear the area of ants in no time at all.

Dishwasher Detergent (powder)

Borax and baking soda can be combined to make a dishwasher detergent that gets your dishes clean and leaves no residue. Since borax helps soften hard water, this detergent also helps minimize hard water stains on dishes and silverware.

INGREDIENTS:

1 cup borax.

1 cup baking soda.

DIRECTIONS:

Mix the borax and baking soda together until they're thoroughly combined. Use by adding a tablespoon or two of this dishwasher detergent to the dishwasher when you're washing your dishes.

Drain Cleaner

Borax can be used as drain cleaner that deodorizes and cleans out clogged drains. This simple recipe allows you to naturally rid your sinks of stubborn clogs without having to resort to caustic chemicals.

INGREDIENTS:

1 cup borax.

2 cups boiling water.

DIRECTIONS:

Add 1 cup of borax to the sink. Let it sit for 20 to 30 minutes. Bring 2 cups of water to a boil and pour it down the sink. Let it sit for an additional 15 minutes and run the water until the drain unclogs.

Flower Preserver

Here's a little known use for borax. It can be used to preserve flowers by pulling the moisture out of them. It can be used on its own, but works best when combined with other natural products to gently dry flowers while preserving color and minimizing shrinkage.

INGREDIENTS:

1 part borax.

2 parts cornmeal or oatmeal.

DIRECTIONS:

Combine the borax and cornmeal or oatmeal. Place a thin layer of the mixture in the bottom of a box large enough to hold the flower(s) you're trying to preserve. Lay the flower(s) down in the box. Cover the flower(s) with the mixture, making sure to completely cover the petals and leaves. Leave the flower(s) in the box until dry.

Be careful not to leave flowers in the box for too long or they'll become brittle and will fall apart when touched.

Rust Remover

Got rust you're looking to get rid of? Make short work of it with this lemon-scented rust remover. It works well on surface rust, but isn't going to do much if the rust is bad enough to cause pitting.

INGREDIENTS:

1 cup borax.

2 cups warm water.

2 tablespoons lemon juice.

DIRECTIONS:

Combine the borax, warm water and lemon juice to make a paste. Rub the paste onto the rusty area and let it sit for 5 minutes. Scrub the paste off and the rust should lift away as well.

Scouring Paste

Some cleaning jobs require an abrasive cleaner capable of scrubbing away tough stains, dirt and grime. You can use this scouring paste to clean toilets, tubs, sinks and tile grout.

INGREDIENTS:

½ cup borax.

½ cup baking soda.

2 cups hot water.

DIRECTIONS:

Combine the borax and baking soda. Add hot water and slowly stir it in until the mixture is the consistency you want it. Use a sponge or scouring pad combined with this paste to clean toilets, tubs and sinks. Apply the paste to dirty tile grout and let it sit for 15 minutes. Scrub it away with a stiff plastic brush.

Sink Stain Remover

Use this recipe to remove stubborn stains from stainless steel and porcelain sinks alike. It can also be used to clean porcelain tubs and toilets.

INGREDIENTS:

2 cups borax.

½ cup lemon juice.

4 drops eucalyptus essential oil.

DIRECTIONS:

Combine the borax and lemon juice to make a paste. Stir in the eucalyptus oil. Use a sponge or cleaning cloth to rub the paste into the stains. With a little elbow grease, most stains will wipe away.

Castile Soap

Castile soap is a vegetable oil-based soap named after a similar type of soap made in the Castile region of Spain. It's made strictly with vegetable fats and is generally considered a high quality soap because it's gentle on the skin and is all-natural. It's usually made from olive oil, but can be made from coconut oil, hemp oil, almond oil or pretty much any other vegetable oil.

Since castile soap is made completely from natural ingredients, it's biodegradable and is considered a green cleaner. It's every bit as effective as synthetic soaps, so for most people making the switch is a no brainer.

Castile soap is sold in both solid and liquid form, but it's the liquid form of castile soap that's used in most natural cleaning recipes. It's unscented in its natural state, but some manufacturers add scent to the soap before packaging it. Avoid scented versions when making natural cleaning products. You can add your own scent in the form of essential oils.

Making Liquid Castile Soap from Bar Soap

Castile soap is easy to find in bar form, but the liquid version may prove difficult to source. When you do find it, sticker shock may ensue, as it tends to carry a hefty price tag. You can make liquid castile soap out of bar castile soap in a few easy steps, saving a decent amount of money in the process.

In order to make liquid castile soap, you're going to need the following items:

- 2 bars of castile soap.
- ½ gallon of distilled water.
- A vegetable grater.
- A large pot.

Follow these directions to make liquid castile soap:

1. Grate the bars of castile soap. If you're feeling lazy, you can chop the castile soap up using your blender, but it's soft enough a grater will make short work of it.
2. Place the water in the pot and bring it to a boil.
3. Turn off the heat and add the castile soap.
4. Give it a good stir and leave the soap in the hot water for 45 minutes to an hour. The soap will dissolve into the water.
5. Stir it one last time and bottle it up. You now have homemade liquid castile soap.

This liquid soap may solidify into a gel or a semi-solid substance in cool temperatures, depending on the type of vegetable oils used to make the castile soap. This is normal.

Gently warm the bottle up by running it under hot water to return the soap to its liquid form.

Uses for Castile Soap

Here are some of the many ways castile soap can be used in the home:

- **Mix it with water in a 1:4 ratio and use it as shampoo.**
- **Add a couple tablespoons of liquid castile soap to a bucket of water and use it to mop the floors.**
- **Diluted castile soap can be used to clean eyeglasses and sunglasses without streaking.**
- **Spray castile soap on your shoes and scrub them with a toothbrush to return them to like new condition.**
- **Use full-strength castile soap to cut through grease for the tougher cleaning jobs.**

Liquid castile soap can be used on its own for all sorts of cleaning jobs. Add a teaspoon or two to a quart of water for light cleaning jobs, dilute it 1:1 with water for tougher cleaning jobs and use it at full strength when you need serious cleaning power.

Castile Soap Recipes

Before we get into the recipes for castile soap, there's one thing I want to let you know. Castile soap is different from the soaps you're probably used to in that cleaning products made with castile soap don't suds up like the synthetic soaps you're used to.

The suds in many commercial products are meaningless and the synthetic chemicals that are added to the products to cause them aren't there to make the product more effective. They're added to fool the consumer into thinking the products are more effective. You see the suds and assume the product is working. The products bubble and foam because manufacturers know you want to see them bubble and foam.

Castile soap recipes may have a few bubbles, but they don't include the unnecessary sudsing agents found in commercial products. You won't get the same bubbles, but your house and clothes will still get clean. The lack of bubbles in natural cleaning products takes some getting used to, but rest assured you don't need suds to have a clean house.

All-Purpose Cleaner

This recipe combines the powers of baking soda, castile soap and borax all in one cleaner. It's also antibacterial and will help kill germs on the surfaces it comes in contact with.

INGREDIENTS:

½ cup baking soda.

½ cup borax.

5 tablespoons vinegar.

1 cup liquid castile soap.

10 to 20 drops of essential oils (Lemon, lavender and tea tree oil are all good choices.

4 cups water.

DIRECTIONS:

Combine the ingredients in a spray bottle and shake it up. Spray the cleaner on the surface you want to clean. Wipe it down with a clean cloth.

Antibacterial Hand Soap

This hand soap smells great and is antibacterial because of the essential oils added to it. If you dispense it from a foaming soap dispenser, you'll have an all-natural version of foaming hand soap.

INGREDIENTS:

3 tablespoons liquid castile soap.

1 cup distilled water.

1 teaspoon vitamin E oil.

5 drops lavender essential oil.

3 drops tea tree essential oil.

DIRECTIONS:

Combine the ingredients in a bottle and shake until blended. Use as you would regular hand soap.

Dish Soap (Liquid)

Here's a quick and easy dish soap recipe that can be used when washing dishes by hand.

You may have seen "green" recipes online that call for using commercial dish soaps and thought they were natural. While they may be gentle on the hands and better for the environment than some synthetic soaps, dish soaps are often made from petroleum products and contain synthetic fragrances. Not exactly what I want in my natural products.

This dish soap is a much better solution, as it actually is a natural product.

INGREDIENTS:

2 cups liquid castile soap.

5 tablespoons water.

5 to 10 drops antibacterial essential oil (lemon or tea tree oil work well).

DIRECTIONS:

Combine the ingredients in a bottle and shake until blended. Use as you would regular dish soap.

Dishwasher Detergent (Liquid)

There is a recipe for powdered dishwasher detergent in the chapter on Borax. Here's a recipe for liquid dishwasher detergent for those who prefer it.

This recipe is designed to work in homes with hard water. If you find the detergent is leaving a filmy residue or spots on your dishes and silverware, try adding white vinegar to the rinse reservoir on your dishwasher. It will cut through the hard water stains and leave your dishes spot-free and sparkling clean.

This soap will separate during storage. Shake the container you're storing it in to blend it before using it.

INGREDIENTS:

½ cup liquid castile soap.

2 cups water.

1 cup white vinegar.

2 tablespoons washing soda.

2 tablespoons fresh lemon juice.

3 tablespoons salt.

10 drops lemon or tea tree essential oil.

DIRECTIONS:

Add the water, castile soap and white vinegar to a saucepan and heat it up to a boil. Back off until the liquid is simmering. Add the washing soda, lemon juice and salt and stir them in until they dissolve. Turn off the heat and let the detergent cool before adding the essential oil. Use a couple tablespoons per load of laundry.

Laundry Soap (Powdered)

Because of the health concerns associated with borax, people tend to be concerned with washing their clothes with natural products containing borax. The amount of borax that makes it through the rinse cycle and comes in contact with the skin is likely very small and of little concern. Besides, if you're currently using commercial laundry soap, this soap is a better alternative to the sulfates, phenols and other chemicals found in synthetic detergents.

This powdered soap is safe to use in HE washing machines because it doesn't have a lot of suds. Note that this recipe calls for grated bar soap instead of liquid castile soap.

INGREDIENTS:

4 cups borax.

4 cups washing soda.

2 cups finely-grated castile bar soap.

4 tablespoons baking soda.

DIRECTIONS:

Combine all of the ingredients in a large bowl and stir them until they're thoroughly mixed. Add ¼ cup of this detergent to your laundry.

Laundry Soap (Liquid)

Here's a liquid version of the soap from the previous recipe. This liquid soap is safe to use in HE washing machines.

INGREDIENTS:

2 cups borax.

1 cup vinegar.

1 cup washing soda.

½ cup liquid castile soap.

8 cups water.

DIRECTIONS:

Bring 8 cups of water and the vinegar to a boil on the stove. Stir in the liquid castile soap, washing soda and the borax and stir it until it's dissolved. Let the soap mixture sit for at least 12 hours. Pour it into gallon jugs and place the lids on the jugs. Shake the jugs until the soap mixture is blended. Use ¾ to 1 cup of this soap with each load of laundry.

Oven Cleaner

Commercial oven cleaners are often filled with caustic chemicals that are a hazard to anyone who comes in contact with them or their fumes. This oven cleaner is a much safer alternative that'll cut grease and grime and leave your oven clean and smelling great.

INGREDIENTS:

½ cup washing soda.

1 cup liquid castile soap.

5 to 10 drops eucalyptus essential oil.

DIRECTIONS:

Combine all of the ingredients into a paste. Apply the paste to your oven and let it sit for half an hour to 45 minutes. Scrub away the paste.

Tub and Tile Cleaner

This gentle cleaner will allow you to effortlessly scrub away dirt and grime from your tub, your shower and your tile counters. If you've got extremely dirty grout, use the grout cleaner in the hydrogen peroxide chapter after cleaning the tile with this recipe.

INGREDIENTS:

1 cup liquid castile soap.

3 cups water.

1 cup baking soda.

DIRECTIONS:

Place the castile soap and water in a spray bottle and shake until blended. Sprinkle baking soda liberally over the area you're going to clean. Spray the castile soap solution onto the baking soda and scrub with a scrub brush or a sponge.

Window Cleaner

Because they're made of glass, windows are relatively easy to clean. What isn't so easy is making sure windows are free of streaks once dry. Use this recipe and the instructions below to ensure your windows are crystal clear and free of streaking.

INGREDIENTS:

2 teaspoons liquid Castile soap.

½ cup vinegar.

3 cups water.

DIRECTIONS:

Combine all ingredients in a spray bottle and shake the bottle to blend them together. Lightly mist the window you're cleaning and wipe it down with a newspaper.

Hydrogen Peroxide

If your family is anything like the average Western family, you have a bottle or two of hydrogen peroxide tucked away in the medicine cabinet. When someone gets a minor injury that needs cleaning, you reach for the bottle of hydrogen peroxide to disinfect the wound with its gentle bubbling action. The hydrogen peroxide is then returned to the cabinet, where it's forgotten until the next time it's needed to clean a cut, scrape or burn.

It might surprise you to hear that familiar brown bottle in your cabinet contains a simple peroxide liquid that's capable of much more than just cleaning wounds. It can be used for a number of green cleaning applications and is a diverse tool that you're going to want in your arsenal.

Apply hydrogen peroxide to a dirty surface and it'll instantly go to work. You'll be able to see it bubbling as it makes short work of bacteria, pathogens, mold spores, fungus and all sorts of harmful microorganisms. Let it sit on a surface for 30 seconds before wiping it away and you can rest assured you've just eliminated a good amount of the bacteria on that surface.

You can buy hydrogen peroxide in a number of strengths, ranging from 3% to 30% or more. All you'll need for cleaning purposes is the 3% solution. Anything more than that is usually overkill and hydrogen peroxide can be highly caustic in larger concentrations. Some people prefer purchasing stronger concentrations and diluting it themselves, but this practice is best left to those who know exactly what they're doing. Stick to the 3% solution sold in pharmacies and drug stores and you'll be good to go.

Exposure to light causes hydrogen peroxide to quickly break down. Store it in a dark bottle in a dark area of the house to ensure it lasts as long as possible.

Uses for Hydrogen Peroxide

Hydrogen peroxide alone is a powerful oxidative cleaner. Here are some of the ways hydrogen peroxide can be used on its own:

- **Use a solution of half water and half hydrogen peroxide to rinse off fruit and vegetables.** This solution will kill off E. coli and salmonella bacteria.
- **Hydrogen peroxide can be used to clean and deodorize kitty litter boxes.** Dump out the litter and saturate the bottom and sides of the box with hydrogen peroxide. Let it sit for 45 minutes and then scrub the box out and rinse it.
- **Add a cup of 3% peroxide to your laundry to brighten whites and remove yellow stains from white linens.**
- **Remove bloodstains by blotting stained clothing with peroxide and washing it out with cold water after letting it sit for a minute or two.**
- **Clean flat surfaces in the house with peroxide to kill bacteria.**
- **Use hydrogen peroxide to clean windows, mirrors and glass without leaving streaks.**

Hydrogen Peroxide Recipes

Hydrogen peroxide is used in applications where sanitization is of concern. It kills microorganisms through oxidation. The following recipes use the oxidative properties of hydrogen peroxide to clean and disinfect the surfaces they're applied to.

Disinfectant Spray

Use this disinfectant spray to remove germs and bacteria from almost any surface. It's important to keep the vinegar and hydrogen peroxide in separate bottles until you're ready to use them. This spray is safe to use on food preparation surfaces and can even be used to clean fruits and vegetables.

INGREDIENTS:

2 cups vinegar.

2 cups 3% hydrogen peroxide.

DIRECTIONS:

Place the vinegar and hydrogen peroxide into separate spray bottles. Spray one of the bottles onto the surface you plan on cleaning and follow it up by spraying the other bottle on the same area. It doesn't matter which of the bottles you spray first. Wipe the vinegar and hydrogen peroxide away.

Barbecue Grill Cleaner

My husband does all the barbecuing in our house. It's the only time I can get him to cook, so I'm all for it. What he doesn't do a very good job of is cleaning the grill after cooking. I made the mistake of looking at the grill last time he was cooking on it and I was disgusted by what I found. Layers of grease and grime that obviously hadn't been cleaned in quite some time caked the grill and the burners beneath it.

I struggled to find a cleaning solution that worked to lift the grease and grime until I stumbled across this one. It cut right through the grease and allowed me to finish cleaning the grill in no time at all.

INGREDIENTS:

1 cup hydrogen peroxide.

2 cups baking soda.

DIRECTIONS:

Add hydrogen peroxide to the baking soda to create a paste. Apply the paste liberally to the grill and let it sit for 15 to 20 minutes. Scrub it clean with a scouring pad.

Grout Cleaner

Grout can be difficult to keep clean, especially if spills aren't wiped up right away. If you have kids or a spouse who doesn't pay attention to what they're doing, you know exactly what I mean. Cleaning stubborn stains requires a lot of elbow grease. This grout cleaner isn't going to completely eliminate the scrubbing, but it should make life a bit easier on you, as it's an effective cleaner that lifts stains out of the grout it's used on.

INGREDIENTS:

½ cup baking soda.

3 tablespoons of water.

½ cup hydrogen peroxide.

DIRECTIONS:

Combine the baking soda and water to create a paste. Apply the paste to the grout and let it sit for 5 minutes. Place the hydrogen peroxide into a spray bottle and spray it onto the baking soda paste. Give it a chance to foam up and then use a toothbrush or a brush with stiff plastic bristles to scrub the grout clean.

Stain Remover

I've got two kids at home and a husband who has a love for anything mechanical. OxiClean used to be my best friend, but it's rather costly to buy when you've got a constant supply of stained clothes in need of stain removal. This stain remover recipe uses hydrogen peroxide and washing soda to effectively and inexpensively lift stains out of clothing.

For best results, mix the ingredients right before using them. I've found this recipe is most effective when a fresh bottle of hydrogen peroxide is used. If you use a bottle that's been sitting around for a while, it doesn't seem to work as well.

Be aware this stain remover has the potential to cause fading. Test it on an inconspicuous area prior to applying it to larger areas.

INGREDIENTS:

¼ cup washing soda.

½ cup water.

¼ cup hydrogen peroxide.

DIRECTIONS:

Combine the ingredients in a spray bottle and mix them together. Spray the stain remover on the stain you're attempting to remove. Let the clothes sit for 30 minutes before running the clothes through the washing machine.

Whitening Toothpaste

Brand name toothpastes are packed full of chemical cleaners and foaming agents that can be harmful if swallowed. Brushing your teeth 2 to 3 times a day using these chemicals sounds like a really bad idea. Since you can't just ignore dental care, try this all-natural toothpaste instead.

INGREDIENTS:

½ cup hydrogen peroxide.

1 cup baking soda.

½ cup warm water.

A few drops of peppermint essential oil.

DIRECTIONS:

Combine all of the ingredients and add water until they form a thick paste. Dip your toothbrush into the paste and proceed to brush your teeth.

Salt

I'm a big fan of natural home cleaning solutions that serve double duty in the kitchen. While vinegar and baking soda are well-known in the natural cleaning community, you don't hear a whole lot about salt. This is a bit strange, because there are certain applications where salt is an effective cleaner, both on its own and when combined with other natural cleaners.

The type of salt you use doesn't matter, but additive-free salts like unrefined sea salt, canning salt or most kosher salts are the better choice for the environment because they don't contain anti-caking agents. You don't have to spend a ton of money on the best of the best Himalayan sea salts for cleaning purposes. Save those salts for the culinary recipes where they really matter.

Uses for Salt

Salt alone can be used for the following household cleaning purposes:

- **Sprinkle a light coating of salt onto pans in which you've just fried foods to help keep the black crispy stuff from sticking to the pan.** This will make cleaning easier later on when you decide to clean the pan.
- **Fill your coffee maker's pot with water and add a couple tablespoons of salt to it.** Bring the water to a boil to remove water and coffee stains.
- **Dip sponges in a saltwater solution after cleaning with them to keep them fresh.**
- **Clean up spilled wine by blotting up as much as you can get and then sprinkling salt over what's left.** The salt will pull the wine out of the carpet or linen. Vacuum the salt out of carpet or wash it out of linen with cold water.
- **Wash faded linens or curtains in a saltwater solution to restore their color.**
- **Keep a box of salt handy to use to put out grease fires.**
- **Sprinkle rock salt on your driveway and any walkways you want to keep clear of ice and snow.** The rock salt will prevent the ice and snow from building up and will make it easier to remove.

Salt Recipes

Salt was in use in the home long before modern chemical cleaners were invented. Many of the recipes in this chapter date back hundreds, if not thousands of years. These uses have withstood the test of time and are every bit as valid today as they were when they were in widespread use many years ago.

Salt is a great cleaning agent that really comes into its own when combined with other natural ingredients. One area where salt really shines is when it's combined with vinegar to make a potent cleaner that can be used on difficult stains and mineral deposits. When vinegar alone won't get the job done, try adding a tablespoon or two of salt to boost the cleaning power of the vinegar.

Brass and Copper Cleaner

Here's a recipe designed to leave your brass and copper items clean and clear. This cleaner works well on lightly tarnished brass and copper. It can be used on badly tarnished copper, but may not completely clean it up. It will, however, usually get it a couple shades lighter and remove much of the black oxidation.

INGREDIENTS:

2 tablespoons salt.

½ cup vinegar.

½ cup lemon juice.

DIRECTIONS:

Combine the salt, vinegar and lemon juice. Let the copper or brass items soak in the solution before wiping them clean.

Metal Polish

This polish works to shine most metals, including gold and silver. Always test it on a small area first and wait to see if there's going to be a reaction. If there isn't a reaction, it's probably OK to use it on the item.

INGREDIENTS:

½ cup salt.

½ cup vinegar.

½ cup white flour.

DIRECTIONS:

Combine the ingredients and stir them together to form a paste. Rub it generously onto the metal you're polishing and let it sit for 45 minutes before wiping it away.

Rust Removal Paste

Got rust? Apply this paste to it and the rust will be able to be wiped away a short time later. You'll be surprised at how well it works on surface rust.

INGREDIENTS:

1 cup salt.

¼ cup cream of tartar.

Water.

DIRECTIONS:

Combine the salt and the cream of tartar. Add water and stir it in until the solution is the consistency of thick paste. Apply the paste to the rusty area and let it air-dry. Buff the paste away and the rust should come up with it.

Silver Polish

Silver can take on a black patina as it ages. This silver treatment works well to eliminate the darkening and leaves most silver items nice and shiny.

INGREDIENTS:

½ cup baking soda.

6 tablespoons salt.

8 cups water.

DIRECTIONS:

Add the water to a pot and bring it to a boil. Stir in the baking soda and salt. Place the item you're trying to polish into the pot and let it sit for 30 seconds. Remove from the water and let it cool until it can be handled. Wipe it down with a soft cloth.

Silver Tarnish Remover

Tarnished silver is the result of a chemical reaction between sulfur-containing substances in the air and the surface of the silver itself. The dark material that builds up on the surface is silver sulfide and allowing too much of it to build up can result in silver that appears dark and dull. Silver tarnish remover gets rid of silver sulfide, restoring silver items back to their original luster.

INGREDIENTS:

5 tablespoons salt.

5 tablespoons baking soda.

4 cups water.

Aluminum foil.

DIRECTIONS:

Line a pot with aluminum foil. Add water to the pot and bring it to a boil. Stir in the salt and baking soda. Place the silver item in the pot and let it boil for 5 to 10 minutes. Remove the pot from the heat and let the item cool before wiping it dry.

Oven Spill Cleaner

Spills happen. If you cook frequently, you're bound to spill something in your oven sooner or later. This oven spill cleaner not only helps you clean up the spill, it leaves your kitchen smelling like cinnamon instead of burnt food.

INGREDIENTS:

½ cup salt.

1 tablespoon cinnamon.

DIRECTIONS:

Combine the salt and cinnamon and mix thoroughly. Sprinkle the mixture generously onto the spill as soon as it happens and let the oven cool. Wipe away the spilled food.

Pot and Pan Cleaner

Cast iron pots and pans occasionally need a good deep cleaning. This solution works wonders on the baked-on grease and grime that's par for the course with cast iron cookware. I've used it to clean my own pots and pans and have used it on cookware I've purchased from the thrift store to give it new life.

INGREDIENTS:

½ cup cooking oil.

¼ cup sea salt.

DIRECTIONS:

Pour the oil into the pot or pan and gently heat it. Add the salt and stir it in until it forms a paste. Scrub the pot or pan with the cleaner and rinse it with hot water.

Wood Polish

This polish combines olive oil and vinegar with a bit of salt to create polish that not only leaves wood shiny and smooth; it can even temporarily fill in small nicks and light scratches.

INGREDIENTS:

3 tablespoons sea salt.

1 cup olive oil.

½ cup white vinegar.

DIRECTIONS:

Combine the ingredients in a spray bottle and shake the bottle until they're blended. Spray the polish onto a soft cloth and work it into the wood. Let it sit for 5 minutes and then wipe it away with a clean cloth.

Vinegar

There are two types of vinegar commonly used for cleaning:

- **Apple cider vinegar.**
- **Distilled white vinegar.**

While there are differences in both the flavor and medical benefits between apple cider vinegar and white vinegar, when it comes time to choose vinegar for culinary dishes, both vinegars are pretty much on equal ground. Distilled white vinegar is cheaper than apple cider vinegar, so it may be the better choice for budget-conscious green cleaners.

The key difference between the two when it comes to cleaning is the smell. Apple cider vinegar has a more pleasant smell than white vinegar, so I turn to ACV whenever smell is of concern.

Uses for Vinegar

The **acetic acid** in vinegar is strongly antibacterial and antifungal. Vinegar alone can be used to disinfect and clean a number of surfaces in the house. You can use vinegar to clean the following items:

- **Bathtubs.**
- **Brass.**
- **Coffee pots.**
- **Dishes.**
- **Dishwashers.**
- **Enamel.**
- **Glass.**
- **Ovens and microwaves.**
- **Porcelain.**
- **Refrigerators.**
- **Showers.**
- **Tile.**
- **Toilets.**
- **Windows.**

Vinegar can also be added to the fabric softener reservoir of your washing machine to keep clothes nice and soft. Check the owner's manual for your washer. The rubber hoses on some washing machines may not play nice with vinegar.

Strong odors in the house can be difficult to get rid of. Vinegar has deodorant properties that allow it to be used to neutralize most household odors. Place vinegar in a spray bottle and spray it on areas of the house with odors you want to get rid of. Alternatively, you can wipe the area down with a cloth rag soaked in vinegar. Some smells can even be eliminated by leaving a bowl or pan full of vinegar sitting in the room.

Vinegar Recipes

Vinegar works great as a standalone cleaner. It works even better when combined with other natural products to create natural cleaners that can be used for all sorts of household tasks.

The following green cleaning ingredients are commonly combined with vinegar:

- **Salt.**
- **Baking soda.**
- **Hydrogen peroxide.**
- **Borax.**

It's important to note baking soda and vinegar will react with one another when combined, creating a frothy foam. This neutralizes the cleaning power of the vinegar and baking soda after a few minutes, but can be used to create a cleaner that foams up and removes clogs. Never store cleaning solutions that contain both baking soda and vinegar mixed together because they'll be useless when you go to use them.

Vinegar should never be combined with ammonia because it neutralizes the cleaning power of both compounds, creating water and ammonium acetate as a result. Slight amounts of chlorine gas will be released during the reaction, which you really don't want to inhale.

Air Freshener

Spray a commercial air freshener in the air and you'll be rewarded with a fresh scent that smells like flowers or a spring meadow or any variety of other happy smells. You'll also be rewarded with a nose full of chemical scents whipped up in a laboratory somewhere designed to mimic the fresh scent.

This recipe uses essential oils instead of synthetic chemicals to provide a fragrance that has health benefits, as opposed to one that possibly causes health problems. The air will be deodorized and cleaned by the essential oils and the smells will be eliminated instead of masked, which is what happens with synthetic air fresheners.

INGREDIENTS:

1 cup vinegar.

10 to 20 drops of essential oil (lemon, orange and lavender are popular choices).

1 cup water.

DIRECTIONS:

Combine all of the ingredients in a spray bottle. When you want to freshen the air, spray a couple sprays into air in the room you want to freshen.

All-Purpose Cleaner

All-purpose cleaner is as close as you get to a single solution for all of your household cleaning needs. It isn't perfect for every application, but it'll usually get the job done. I've always got a bottle of this stuff sitting around the house. It's safe on most surfaces and is non-toxic to boot.

This solution works great for cleaning tarnished copper. Spray it on the metal and wipe away the copper oxide layer on the copper. Avoid using this spray to clean valuable copper items because each time you use it, a tiny bit of the copper is dissolved away.

INGREDIENTS:

1 cup vinegar.

2 cups water.

DIRECTIONS:

Combine the vinegar and water. Place the all-purpose cleaner in a spray bottle. Spray it onto the surfaces you plan on cleaning and wipe them down with a sponge or a rag.

Carpet Stain Remover

Carpets can be a real hassle to keep clean. If you've got a lighter colored carpet and have children or grandchildren, you know exactly what I mean. Once stains set in, they can be a bear to get out, with some of the tougher stains requiring hours of scrubbing just to make a little headway. Some stains can set into carpet to the point that you'll scrub the carpet down to the backing before the stain comes out.

This stain remover won't completely eliminate scrubbing, but it will help you pull some stains out of your carpet. It won't work on all stains, so use it judiciously.

If your carpet is under warranty, refer to manufacturer's instructions regarding stain removal. This remover has worked on every carpet I've tried it on, but I can't guarantee it'll work on all carpet types. I also can't guarantee it won't void your warranty.

INGREDIENTS:

1 cup vinegar.

4 tablespoons salt.

3 tablespoons borax.

DIRECTIONS:

Combine the borax, vinegar and salt. Rub the mixture into the stain and let the stain remover dry. Vacuum the area once the stain remover has dried. Repeat until the stain is gone.

Coffee Maker Cleaner

If you've ever turned your coffee maker on only to get an excruciatingly slow drip or no drip at all, you've likely fallen victim to mineral deposits. These deposits are common in households with hard water. Minerals in the water build up on the surfaces the water comes in contact with and eventually clog the coffee maker.

Running vinegar through your coffee maker once a month will prevent the buildup of these deposits.

INGREDIENTS:

1 cup vinegar.

4 cups hot water.

DIRECTIONS:

Add the vinegar and hot water to the reservoir of the coffee maker and run it through a normal brewing cycle. Check the coffee maker to make sure it's working properly. If it's still having trouble, run another cycle of vinegar and water through the machine. If it's OK, fill the coffee maker up with water and run it through the brewing process. Cycle water through the coffee maker a couple times to make sure it's clean.

Foaming Drain Cleaner

Foaming drain cleaner works well to unclog drains that are only partially clogged because it works its way into the clog and foams up, breaking the clog loose so it can be washed down the drain. It doesn't work as well on fully clogged drains. Try pouring a couple cups of boiling water down the drain first to see if it partially unclogs the drain.

The gas created by this reaction is harmless carbon dioxide gas.

INGREDIENTS:

1 cup vinegar.

1 cup baking soda

1 cup table salt.

2 cups boiling water.

DIRECTIONS:

Pour the baking soda and salt down the drain. For smaller drains, use ½ a cup of each. Follow the baking soda and salt up by pouring the vinegar down the drain. The mixture will foam up and hopefully unclog the drain. For stubborn clogs, pour boiling water down the drain once the baking soda and vinegar stop foaming. You may have to use this drain cleaner a couple times before the clog breaks free.

Leather Revitalizer

Dull, lifeless leather can sometimes be brought back to life using a combination of vinegar and linseed oil. Test this recipe in a small area first to make sure it works the way you want it to.

INGREDIENTS:

½ cup vinegar.

1 cup linseed oil.

DIRECTIONS:

Mix the vinegar and linseed oil together and place it in a spray bottle. Spray the old leather with a fine mist of the revitalizer and use a cloth to disperse it across the leather. Let it sit for a few minutes and then wipe the revitalizer away.

Mineral Deposit Remover

As hard water dries, it leaves trace amounts of mineral behind. Over time, these minerals can build up and leave white stains on metal fixtures, pots and pans. This mineral deposit remover can be used to remove staining due to hard water mineral deposits.

Shower heads are a common place for hard water mineral deposits. Place this solution in a plastic bag and tie or tape the plastic bag in place. Let the shower head soak for 30 minutes before removing the bag and testing the shower.

INGREDIENTS:

½ cup vinegar.

1 cup water.

3 tablespoons baking soda.

DIRECTIONS:

Combine the vinegar, water and baking soda. Use the mineral deposit remover immediately. Do not store this solution.

Mold Cleaner

Bleach is the most common agent used to neutralize and clean mold in the home. It's effective, but it's also highly toxic and emits strong fumes that can rapidly build up when it's used in a confined area. A combination of borax and vinegar can be used to effectively clean mold off of small areas. Larger wide-spread mold issues are best left to the professionals.

INGREDIENTS:

1 cup vinegar.

1 cup borax.

8 cups water.

5 drops tea tree essential oil.

DIRECTIONS:

Combine all of the ingredients. Use a rag or sponge to scrub the moldy area until the mold has been scrubbed away. Alternatively, place the mold cleaner into a spray bottle and spray it onto the moldy area. Let it sit for 10 minutes before scrubbing it away.

There's no need to clean the mold cleaner off the surface of the material being cleaned. The borax and vinegar will act as a natural deterrent to new mold growth.

Wood Revitalizer

Do you have wood in your house that's starting to fade and looks dull and lifeless? If so, this revitalizer may be able to bring it back to life.

INGREDIENTS:

3 tablespoons vinegar.

1 tablespoon jojoba oil.

10 drops lemon essential oil.

DIRECTIONS:

Combine all 3 ingredients in a container and cap the container. Shake the container until the contents are blended. Rub a small amount of the revitalizer into the wood and let it sit for 5 minutes. Use a clean cloth to wipe away any oily residue.

Wood Scratch Remover

Technically, this scratch remover doesn't actually remove scratches in wood. It does make them less visible, which can extend the life of your wood furniture and cabinets. Be sure to test this product on a small area first to make sure it has the desired effect. It works better on some types of wood than it does on others.

INGREDIENTS:

1 cup vinegar.

Iodine.

DIRECTIONS:

Combine vinegar and iodine to make this wood scratch remover. The amount of iodine used is dependent on the type of wood you're attempting to remove scratches from. Lighter woods will require small amounts of iodine, while darker wood will require a larger amount. Be forewarned it's tough to get the color just right.

Cleaning Specific Areas of the House

Now that you have a bunch of recipes at your disposal, we're going to switch things up and look at natural ways you can clean specific areas of your house. There may be a bit of overlap between the information in this chapter and the recipes found in previous chapters, but it's gathered in a manner you'll find useful when cleaning a specific area of the house.

Don't assume all of the information in this chapter is going to be a repeat of previous chapters. Some of the green cleaning idea and recipes included in this section weren't included in previous chapters.

Flooring and Carpet

No matter what room in the house you're cleaning, you're going to have a floor. I know, I know. This is a bit surprising, but I assure you there's going to be a floor in every room.

There are thousands of brands and types of flooring found in homes across the nation. Tile, hardwood, carpet, linoleum. The list goes on and on. The tips in this chapter are tailored to encompass large groups of flooring like wood floors or tile floors. Entire books could, and have, been written on just a single type of flooring. For this reason, the recipes and tips in this chapter may not be suited to the individual type of flooring in your house. It's up to you to determine whether or not they're a good fit.

If in doubt, test them on a small area before using them on your entire floor. That way, any damage is limited to a small section of flooring.

Carpet

Most homes have carpet somewhere in the home. Light-colored carpets look great while they're new, but soon fall victim to dirty feet and children and can start to look grungy amazingly fast, even if you vacuum regularly. When your carpet starts to look dirty, you may be tempted to turn to chemical carpet cleaning products, but rest assured there are natural alternatives that are much safer and every bit as effective.

Vacuuming your carpet regularly will get rid of accumulated dirt, dust and particulate matter before it gets ground into the carpet. Try sweeping your carpet with a broom with stiff bristles before vacuuming it in order to make the fibers stand up. As carpet gets walked on, the fibers get compressed, trapping dirt below the top layer of carpet. Sweeping the carpet opens it up, allowing the vacuum to pull dirt from deep within the carpet.

Natural dry shampoo can be added to carpet to deodorize it and help pull dirt out of the carpet during vacuuming. Combine the following ingredients and sprinkle the dry shampoo across your carpet:

- 2 cups baking soda.
- 1 cup cornstarch.
- 2 tablespoons ground cloves.

This dry shampoo won't just help clean your carpet. It'll leave it smelling great. A cup of borax can be added if the carpet is really stinky. Some people like to add baby powder to their carpet for an even better smell, but the fine particles in baby powder are difficult to vacuum up and can build up over time. Also be aware that using dry shampoos that contain any kind of powder can damage your vacuum cleaner as they build up in the inner workings over time.

Carpet stain remover can be made by mixing the following ingredients:

- 1 cup vinegar.
- 4 tablespoons salt.
- 3 tablespoons borax.

Spray it onto the stain and wait 30 minutes before blotting it up. Don't use it to remove anything with dyes in it from your carpet as the vinegar might have the opposite effect and end up setting the dye into the carpet. You can also mix equal parts club soda and corn starch to make stain remover. Hydrogen peroxide may be able to be used to lift stains out of light carpet, but bleaching may be a concern.

For larger stains that are difficult to remove, try a carpet cleaning machine that uses steam to clean the carpet. A solution of half vinegar and half water can be added to most carpet cleaners, but check with the rental company first.

Hardwood Floors

Hardwood floors are one of the more difficult types of flooring to keep shiny and clean. Commercial cleaners tend to build up into a glaze on hardwood floors, leaving them looking dull and lifeless. The glaze then collects dirt which makes them harder to clean because no matter how much scrubbing you do, your floors don't look clean.

Sometimes the simplest solutions are the best ones and when it comes to finished hardwood floors, it's tough to beat the following **wood floor cleaner**:

- Half a cup of vinegar
- A gallon of water.
- ¼ cup castile soap.

Mix the ingredients in a bucket and either get on your hands and knees and start scrubbing or use a mop and bucket to damp mop the floor. Damp mopping uses a mop that's been dipped in the cleaner and then wrung out so it's barely wet. Don't leave the floor wet after cleaning. There shouldn't be any standing water left to pool up on the floor. If you have difficulty handling the smell of the vinegar, try adding a few drops of lemon essential oil to the bucket.

To polish finished hardwood floors and leave them nice and shiny, try this recipe for **wood floor polish**:

- ¼ cup vegetable oil (I prefer olive oil).
- 3 tablespoons vinegar.

- 2 tablespoons vodka.

If the above polish doesn't get the job done, try adding a couple tablespoons of fresh lemon juice to the polish.

Wood floor polish can also be created by soaking 2 green tea bags in a quart of boiling water for 10 minutes. Add 5 to 10 drops of lemon essential oil to the tea and polish the floor as you normally would.

The above solutions aren't a good choice for waxed hardwood, as they can cut through the wax on the floor. To create a **natural wood floor wax** that can be used on most waxed wood surfaces, gather the following ingredients:

- ½ cup almond oil.
- ½ cup vodka.
- 3 tablespoons palm wax.
- 3 tablespoons bees wax, grated.

Melt the beeswax and palm wax in a pot and stir in the almond oil and vodka. Let the mixture harden back into wax and apply the wax by rubbing it into the wood. Test on a small area first, as this wax may not be a good fit for all wood floors.

Water spilled on wood floors will leave white spots when it dries. Fine steel wool and a blend of citrus essential oil and jojoba oil can be used to buff out these water marks.

Kids and pets can really do a number on hardwood floors. Scuff marks can usually be removed by sprinkling baking soda on a damp rag or sponge and rubbing them out. Scratches, dents and dings can be fixed by using a color crayon that's a close match to fill in the damaged areas and then heating the crayon with a blow dryer. Rub the area gently with a soft cloth to help blend the crayon in.

Laminate Floors

Laminate flooring looks like wood, but is actually made of four layers of material designed to capture the look of wood while being more durable. Here are the four layers you'll find in most laminate floors:

- **The backing is the bottom layer.** It acts as a moisture barrier between the flooring and the ground it's laid on.
- **The inner core layer is made of pressed wood fibers that are fused with resin to create a strong, dense material.**
- **The design layer is a picture of actual wood that's laid over the inner core.** This is the layer you see that looks like real wood.
- **The wear layer is a clear topcoat that protects the design layer from damage.**

This type of flooring is easy to clean. Many manufacturers call for using specific cleaning solutions sold by that manufacturer. These solutions are typically expensive chemical cleaning solutions. You don't need these solutions to clean a laminate floor. All you usually need is a dust mop or a vacuum cleaner. For tougher spills or stains, wipe the floor with a damp sponge or soft cloth.

Do not attempt to wax or polish laminate floors, as they aren't wood and can be damaged by wax and polish. Steer clear of abrasive cleaners and never use steel wool on laminate flooring. If you need a stronger **laminate floor cleaner** than water alone, try the following recipe:

- 2 cups water.

- 2 cups white vinegar.
- ¼ cup castile soap.
- 5 to 10 drops of lavender and tea tree essential oils.

This recipe will get your floors clean and leave your house smelling great.

Linoleum

Linoleum has been in existence for more than a hundred years. It was huge in the 50's and 60's, but fell out of favor in the 70's and 80's. It's seen something of a revival due to the recent "green" craze.

While linoleum looks similar to synthetic vinyl flooring, it's made from natural materials like linseed oil, natural resins, limestone and wood powder. The materials are combined to create "cement" that's rolled then rolled through a machine to make it flat. The flat linoleum is then cured and a protective finish is applied.

The downside to linoleum is it isn't as durable as vinyl. High pH or abrasive cleaners will wear down the protective coating, eventually breaching the coating and causing the linoleum to fade and crack.

As you would with vinyl, dust or vacuum linoleum floors before washing them. Always turn the beater bar on your vacuum off. The best natural **linoleum floor cleaner** is a solution of apple cider vinegar and water. Add a cup of vinegar to a quart of water and use the solution to damp mop the floor. You can also use a cotton cloth to wipe down difficult to clean spots and stains. If the floor is really dirty, you can add half a cup of baking soda to the recipe. It can be scented with 10 – 15 drops of lemon or tea tree essential oil.

For stains the above solution doesn't get out, combine equal parts water and baking soda to create **linoleum stain removal paste**. Apply the paste directly to the stain and scrub it away with a soft cloth.

Marble

There's no doubt marble flooring is beautiful, but it's one of the most difficult types of flooring to maintain because of how soft and porous it is. It stains easily and can fall victim to scratching, chips and dings.

To top things off, you can't use acidic cleaners on marble because the acid can etch into the marble, changing the look and texture of the floor. Cleaning solutions containing lemon, vinegar or other acids should never be used on marble floors because they can cause permanent damage to the floor.

Gentle dusting or dry mopping will keep marble free of dirt and dust. This should be done once a day, preferably in the evening to remove dirt and dust that built up during the day. Every few days, damp mop the marble with water alone. Make sure you don't use too much water. The marble should be dry when you're done damp mopping it or you might end up with white stains on the marble that are tough to remove.

Spills should be wiped up immediately. Leave a spill sitting on marble for too long and it will set into the stone, making cleaning much more difficult. **Marble cleaning solution** can be made by combining the following ingredients:

- 1 tablespoon castile soap.
- 1 quart warm water.

Wash the marble with this solution and then rinse it with clean water. Dry the marble after rinsing it off. This solution can be used to damp mop really dirty marble, but shouldn't be left on the marble. Marble can also be cleaned using a solution of equal parts baking soda and water.

Marble is relatively easy to scratch because of how soft it is. You may be able to lift small scratches from marble using 0000 steel wool. Larger scratches are best left to the professionals.

Tile Floors

Tile floors can be difficult to clean because of the grooves between the tiles. If you start off by mopping or wet cleaning tile floors, you can make the overall cleaning job more difficult by moving dirt and grime into the grout where it'll be harder to clean.

Always start by dry or damp mopping tile floors. This will lift up surface dirt and remove much of the grime from the tiles without transferring the dirt into the grout. Follow this up with a warm water mopping that saturates the tile. For dirty tile, try adding a cup of vinegar to 2 quarts of water to increase the cleaning power.

Scuffs can be removed from tile using a magic eraser or by dipping a sponge in coconut or jojoba oil and rubbing out the scuff. It's going to take some elbow grease to get the tougher scuffs out of porous tile, but it can be done.

Save the grout for last because this is where much of the built-up dirt and grime you wash from tiles themselves will end up. A good grout brush with a long handle can be an invaluable tool in homes with vast expanses of tile flooring. You'll be a lot more comfortable standing and scrubbing the grout with a grout brush than you will on your hands and knees with a toothbrush. This may sound counterintuitive, but the softer-bristled brushes seem to work better than the brushes with stiff bristles.

A simple **grout cleaning paste** can be made by combines 2 cups of baking soda with one cup of water and blending it into a paste. Apply the paste to the grout and let it sit for 15 minutes before scrubbing the grout clean. For tougher grout cleaning jobs, try creating a paste from the following ingredients:

- ½ cup vinegar.
- ½ cup baking soda.
- ½ cup salt.

Apply the cleaner to the grout while it's foaming and let it sit for 15 minutes before scrubbing the grout. This cleaner works well on grout, but shouldn't be used on tile that's sensitive to acid like travertine tile or marble.

Mold and mildew can be a problem with lighter colored grouts and can cause them to become dark and discolored. Create a **grout mold cleaning paste** by combining 3 cups of baking soda with 1 cup of hydrogen peroxide and applying it to the grout. Let it sit for 20 minutes before scrubbing the grout clean. This recipe can bleach colored grout, so use it judiciously.

Sometimes grout won't get clean no matter what you try. When stains are too deep into the grout to remove by scrubbing, you may be able to use fine grit sandpaper to remove the stain. Fold the sandpaper up and sand the grout away until the stain is gone. Be careful not to go too deep and be aware this is a destructive method of cleaning grout and shouldn't be used too often.

Cleaning grout can be made much easier if you seal the grout once it's clean. Sealing grout prevents stains from setting into the grout and keeps spills on the surface. A **natural grout sealer** can be created using the following ingredients:

- ¼ cup beeswax.

- 1 cup linseed oil.

Bring the linseed oil to a boil and stir in the beeswax until it's melted. Use a sponge or soft cloth to apply the wax to the grout, taking care not to get it on the tile. Let it dry for a couple hours and wipe off any excess sealant. Wait a day or two and apply another coat. If you use this sealant on floor grout, you're going to need to reapply it every 3 to 6 months.

Vinyl Floors

Vinyl floors are synthetic floors made to withstand the test of time. Vinyl flooring is thin, yet it still manages to be both durable and stain resistant.

The layer of vinyl used on vinyl floors is so thin an additional layer of foam or felt is added as backing. This is what gives vinyl floors their signature "soft" feeling when you walk on them. The wear layer, which is a clear protective coating placed on top of the vinyl, is what determines how durable vinyl flooring is. The thicker the wear layer, the more durable the flooring will be.

Vacuum vinyl floors with the beater bar turned off or sweep them with a broom to get rid of dust and loose particles before you get them wet. Dust or vacuum vinyl floors regularly because dirt and hard particles can remove the finish from vinyl floors if it gets ground into the floor by foot traffic.

A simple **vinyl floor cleaner** can be made by combining a cup of apple cider vinegar with two quarts of water. Damp mop vinyl floors instead of saturating them. This cleaner will get all but the most stubborn of stains out of vinyl flooring.

Certain stains like coffee stains can be difficult to remove from lighter-colored vinyl flooring. Use the following **vinyl flooring stain remover** recipe to remove stains:

- ½ cup baking soda.
- ½ cup white vinegar.

Apply the solution to a sponge or soft cloth and scrub the stain immediately. Wipe the area with a clean cloth to remove the vinegar and baking soda. Alternatively, a paste made of equal parts baking soda and water will also get the job done.

Lift scuffs from vinyl flooring by apply jojoba oil to the scuff and using a soft cloth or towel to buff it out. Mineral spirits can be used on tough stains and scuffs.

Counters

Counters are another item you're going to find in multiple rooms in the house. Bathrooms, offices and the kitchen will all have counters that need to be cleaned. Countertops can be difficult to keep clean because not only do they collect dirt and dust; they also collect clutter. No matter how hard you try, counters always seems to get cluttered as people set items on the counter and forget about them.

In order to clean your counters and keep them that way, you first have to eliminate the clutter that builds up over time. You aren't going to want to clean cluttered counters, as the time required to clean them increases by quite a bit.

Take one counter in your house at a time and completely clear it of clutter. If there are items you want to keep on the counter like fruit bowls, knife blocks and toothbrush holders, designate a spot for those items and make sure they stay in that spot. Everything else should be tucked away out of sight until you need it. Once it's used, it should be returned to its designated home.

Clearing counters of clutter and making a daily effort to keep them clear will really speed up your cleaning tasks. You won't have to clean up days or even weeks' worth of clutter every time you want to wipe the counters down. Make a pass through your entire house at the end of each day and clear any clutter that's accumulated on flat surfaces throughout the day.

The **all-purpose cleaner** from the castile soap section works well on most countertops. In case you forgot, here are the ingredients:

- ½ cup baking soda.
- 5 tablespoons vinegar.
- ½ cup borax.
- 1 cup liquid castile soap.
- 10 to 20 drops of essential oils (Lemon, lavender and tea tree oil are all good choices.
- 4 cups water.

If you have marble countertops or counters that are sensitive to acid, eliminate the vinegar from the recipe.

Let's take a quick look at some of the more common materials countertops are made from and how you can take care of them using natural products.

Granite and Marble

Granite countertops are extremely durable. Granite is formed deep within the surface of the Earth as molten rock is compressed over the course of millions of years. It's one of the hardest rock types known to man and is heat resistant and tough to scratch, chip or break. It comes with a hefty price tag, but will last you a lifetime if you take proper care of it.

A wet rag or towel is usually all that's required to clean granite countertops. Spills should be wiped up immediately because they can stain granite. Stains that aren't set too deep can often be lifted using hot water and a rag. A tablespoon or two of castile soap can be added to a cup of water to create a **granite cleaning solution** that'll allow you to scrub most stains right up.

Add a cup of baking soda to the solution to create a paste that can be used on water-based stains. Add a few tablespoons of hydrogen peroxide to the solution along with the baking soda for oil-based stains. Apply the paste to the countertop and leave it there for up to 24 hours before wiping it away.

Granite counters can be sealed to protect them from staining. I don't know of any natural sealants that work well, so chemical sealant may be your only option. If you do decide to seal your granite counters, make sure they're completely clean. Stains left on the countertop when granite counters are sealed will be locked in forever.

Marble countertops are also made of stone, but they're a softer, more porous stone. They can be cleaned with the same solutions granite countertops can, but be sure to avoid acidic cleaners at all costs. This is good advice for granite as well. While granite isn't as sensitive to acidic solutions as marble, you should still avoid these cleaners as they can eat away the surface of the granite.

Tile

See the instructions for cleaning tile floors. The same cleaning solutions used on tile flooring can be used on tile countertops. For marble tiles, see the section on marble flooring.

Laminate

Laminate countertops are made by laying decorative paper over core paper and then saturating them with resin. The laminate is then bonded to wood substrate, which acts as a backbone for the laminate.

Because they're made of mostly paper, laminate countertops rank amongst the least expensive counters on the market today. When these inexpensive countertops first hit the market many years ago, they were plagued with problems. Because of this, laminate counters have been labeled as being of poor quality, even though modern manufacturing techniques allow manufacturers to create higher-quality laminates.

To create **laminate countertop cleaner**, combine equal parts water and vinegar. Add a few drops of lemon, lavender or tea tree essential oil to the cleaner to give it a fresh scent. For stains that are stuck to the counter, make a **stain removal paste** by combining baking soda and lemon juice. Apply the paste to the stain and let it sit for 20 minutes before scrubbing it away.

Concrete

Once relegated to sidewalks, driveways and patios, concrete has made its way into the kitchen in the form of concrete countertops. These durable countertops can be poured onsite or they can be prefabricated, delivered and installed. There are a wide variety of shapes, colors and design choices available to consumers because concrete counters are made to order.

Concrete countertops have to be sealed occasionally to ensure stains don't set into the porous concrete. Check with the installer to see whether there are natural sealants available for your concrete counters. Pure beeswax can be used to seal some concrete countertops, but it'll have to be reapplied regularly to maintain the seal and waxed countertops can still get stained when spills are left on them.

If you have stains that are already set into the concrete, create a **concrete stain removal paste** by combining the following ingredients:

- 3 tablespoons hydrogen peroxide.
- 1 cup flour.
- ½ cup water.

Combine the ingredients and blend them together to make a paste. Apply the paste to the stain and let it sit until it dries. Wipe the paste away and the stain should come up with it. You may need to repeat the process multiple times for bad stains.

Cleaning concrete countertops is simple. **Concrete countertop cleaner** consists of 3 tablespoons liquid castile soap added to 2 cups of warm water. This should be all you need to keep your concrete countertops clean. Avoid cleaners with acid in them like vinegar and lemon juice because they can etch the concrete.

Wood

Wood butcher blocks and countertops are relatively rare in modern homes, but are fairly common in older homes. Wooden countertops require special care because they're extremely porous and can harbor bacteria in the many cracks and grooves that exists in the wood. Over time, harmful bacteria can build up in wood counters and be transferred to food that comes in contact with them.

The best thing you can do for wood countertops is to keep them clean and dry. Stains will set into the wood quickly and water can soak into wood counters, leaving water stains and white rings behind. Wipe up spills immediately and clean your countertops with a **wood counter cleaner** made of the following ingredients:

- 2 cups warm water.
- 5 tablespoons liquid castile soap.
- 5 drops lemon essential oil.

Once your counters are clean, wipe them dry. Don't leave standing water on the counters.

Nicks, scratches and burn marks are all areas that can harbor harmful microorganisms. These areas can be sanded smooth with light grit sandpaper. Burns can be rubbed out with a combination of sea salt and lemon juice. Deeper-set burns may require some sanding.

Wood counters need to be sealed. All that's usually required to seal wood counters is a small amount of mineral oil, but check with the manufacturer prior to using anything new on your countertops. Counters that can be sealed with mineral oil will have to be resealed every couple months.

The Kitchen and Dining Room

For most people, the kitchen is the most difficult room in the house to keep clean. It's a high traffic area, so clutter tends to build up on the counters and the floors get dirty quickly because of all the foot traffic. It's also the room where food is made, which creates all sorts of opportunities for messes to be made.

The dining room can also get pretty messy, as the dining room table is often the gathering area of the house. It's used for eating, homework, hanging out and all sorts of other activities.

If I could only have one natural cleaning recipe for the kitchen and dining room, I would make this **all-purpose kitchen cleaner**:

- 1 quart warm water.
- 5 tablespoons baking soda.
- 5 tablespoons liquid castile soap.

Combine these ingredients in a spray bottle and shake them up. This cleaner is safe on most surfaces and can even be used to mop the floor.

The Refrigerator

The all-purposed kitchen cleaner we just discussed can be used to wipe down the inside of the fridge. Add 5 more tablespoons of baking soda for good measure. For difficult jobs, substitute washing soda for the baking soda.

Bad odors can quickly take over a fridge and have you wrinkling your nose every time the door is opened. When you notice a bad smell, the first thing you need to do is clean the fridge to get rid of whatever it is that's causing the bad smell.

Lingering smells that stick around after the fridge has been cleaned can be eliminated in a number of ways, including the following:

- **Place an open box of baking soda in the fridge and leave it there.** It will absorb the smells in the fridge.
- **Freshly ground coffee can be spread out on a plate and left in the fridge to deodorize it.**
- **Soak a few cotton balls in vanilla extract and leave them in the fridge for 24 hours.**
- **Make a spray by combining a cup of water with 10 to 15 drops of your favorite essential oil and spray it in the fridge.**
- **Cut a lemon in half and place the lemon in the fridge, cut side up.**
- **Save your citrus peels and place them in a bowl in the fridge.**

Keep your fridge clean and toss out old food at least once a week and you won't have to worry about bad smells very often.

Cabinets

Dirt, grease and grime can really build up on the outside of cabinets, especially the ones close to the stove and the garbage can. Microfiber towels work well on cabinets and can often be used with water alone to give all of the cabinets in the kitchen a quick wipe down.

Make **cabinet cleaner** using the following ingredients:

- 1 quart warm water.
- 1 tablespoon baking soda.
- 2 teaspoons liquid castile soap.
- 2 tablespoons vinegar.
- 5 drops lemon essential oil.

The essential oil is optional, but it adds the smell of lemon to the recipe and has antibacterial properties.

The Sink and Garbage Disposal

Sometimes you want something strongly antibacterial, like when you're cleaning cutting boards or scrubbing the sink. This **antibacterial soap recipe** will kill bacteria and disinfect the items you use it on:

- 2 cups warm water.
- ½ cup castile soap.
- ¼ cup baking soda.
- 10 drops lavender essential oil.
- 10 drops tea tree essential oil.

This recipe can also be used to disinfect and deodorize dirty garbage cans. Another option for cleaning cutting boards is to cut a lemon in half, dip it in baking soda and use it to scrub the board.

If you've got a rotten smell in your kitchen and can't figure out where it's coming from, the garbage disposal is likely the culprit. The garbage disposal can act as a repository for germs and smelly gunk can build up over time. Cut a lemon in half and toss both halves down the disposal. Run water down the disposal and turn it on. This is usually enough to get rid of garbage disposal stench. If not, pour half a box of baking powder down the disposal, chase it with half a cup of vinegar and let it sit for half an hour before running the water and turning the disposal on.

Dishwashing

Dishwashing is universally named as the least enjoyable cleaning task in the kitchen. If you cook a lot, you've got numerous dishes, pots and pans that need to be cleaned on a daily basis. You're going to need a good dishwasher detergent. Luckily, there are a number of effective natural recipes that can be used to wash dishes.

Here's a powdered dishwasher detergent that works great:

- ½ cup citric acid.
- ½ cup washing soda.
- ¼ cup baking soda.
- 5 tablespoons sea salt.

Here's another that's even easier to make:

- 1 cup borax.
- 1 cup baking soda.

If you prefer liquid dishwashing detergent, here's a good one:

- ½ cup liquid castile soap.
- 2 cups water.
- 1 cup white vinegar.
- 2 tablespoons washing soda.
- 2 tablespoons fresh lemon juice.
- 3 tablespoons salt.
- 10 drops lemon or tea tree essential oil.

In addition to cleaning dishes, you're also going to want to clean out your dishwasher every once in a while. This can be accomplished by placing a bowl of white vinegar on the top rack of the dishwasher and running an empty load. The vinegar will clean the dishwasher, removing soap scum and dirt in the process.

The Oven and Microwave

Grease and kitchens go hand in hand. There are a few areas where grease is likely to build up in the kitchen that are going to require a specialized cleaner. The following **natural degreaser** can be used on stovetops, counters (other than wood and marble) and range hoods to cut through grease:

- ½ cup fresh lemon juice.
- ¼ cup castile soap.
- 1 cup water.

Cleaning your oven is going to require a stronger solution. Combine the following ingredients to make **oven cleaner**:

- ½ cup washing soda.
- 1 cup liquid castile soap.
- 5 to 10 drops eucalyptus essential oil.

Apply the cleaner to the inside of the oven and let it sit overnight. Always wear gloves and eye protection when working with this solution.

The microwave requires special attention because by the time most people clean their microwave, food that's splattered on the walls has been cooked time and time again. If you've ever tried to scrub cooked-on food off of microwave walls, you know how difficult it can be. The following natural techniques can be used to make cleaning the microwave easier:

- **Place a bowl of vinegar in the microwave and cook it on high for 4 minutes.** This will soften

the food stuck to the walls and make it easier to clean.
- **Cut a lemon in half and place it face down on a plate in the microwave.** Microwave it for 3 to 4 minutes. Scrub the insides of the microwave to remove the now softened food.

Both of these techniques can create a significant amount of steam, so be careful when you open the door to the microwave.

Coffee Maker

If you're the type who can't go without their morning cup of joe, your coffee maker probably has both hard water and coffee stains.

These can be removed using **coffee maker cleaner** made by combining a cup of vinegar and a quart of water. Let the solution sit in the coffee maker for a while before cleaning it out.

If you've got a K-cup coffee brewer, mineral deposits can build up until they gum up the works and cause your machine to run slowly or not at all. Try running white vinegar through the machine a few cycles to clear up the deposits. Don't forget to run clean water through the system or your next cup of coffee will smell and taste like vinegar.

The Table

The dining room table is an area that often requires special attention because it's usually one of the main gathering areas in the house. Families eat, drink, work and hang out around the table, often leaving a mess in their wake.

The all-purpose cleaner introduced at the beginning of this section works well to clean most tables. If you have a glass table, use a 1:1 solution of vinegar and water instead. If streaking is of concern, clean the table and dry it with newspaper.

Bathroom

The bathroom is a close second to the kitchen when it comes to the amount of time spent on housecleaning. You've got cabinets, sinks and carpet or some other sort of flooring that has to be kept clean. You've also got toilets, showers, a mirror or two and possibly a tub that needs cleaning.

Because of what you do in the bathroom, this is one room you really have to stay on top of or it'll get dirty in a hurry. If you've got kids, you've probably marveled at how fast the bathroom can go from clean to looking like a tornado hit it.

Bathroom counters are another place where clutter tends to gather, so be sure to remove anything that isn't necessary and stay on top of keeping the counters clear of clutter. Other than a toothbrush holder and a soap dish, try to keep the counter clear.

For instructions on cleaning flooring, carpet and counters, see the first two sections in this chapter. For cleaning the sinks and cabinets, refer to the Kitchen and Dining Room section. The same cleaners that are used in the kitchen can be used in the bathroom.

Mirrors

Bathroom mirrors can gather all sorts of icky materials, especially if you have teenagers in the house. I don't know what half the stuff I clean off the mirrors is, and frankly, I don't want to know. I just want it gone.

To clean mirrors, use a 50/50 solution of vinegar to water. You can add a bit of hydrogen peroxide if you'd like, but it isn't necessary. Use a newspaper to wipe the mirrors clean. Using cloth or paper towels tends to leave streaks.

Shower and Tub

Soap scum, dirt, grease and hard water can all combine to create a cleaning nightmare. Since this is an area of the house that's often left wet, mold and mildew can quickly become a problem.

Requiring that the tub and shower be wiped down with a microfiber cloth after each use can help eliminate these problems, but we all know kids and husbands rarely follow the rules. An easier approach is to leave a squeegee in the shower that can be used to quickly wipe down the shower curtain and walls.

For regular cleaning jobs, this **tub and tile cleaner** will get the job done nicely:

- 1 cup liquid castile soap.
- 3 cups water.
- 1 cup baking soda.

Alternatively, you can use this recipe:

- 1 cup vinegar.
- 1 cup water.
- 10 drops lemon essential oil.

The lemon essential oil is optional, but is included to offset the smell of the vinegar.

Stuck-on gunk and grime is going to take something with a little more cleaning power. Try the following **abrasive tub and shower cleaner** for the harder jobs:

- ½ cup baking soda.
- ½ cup borax.

- ½ cup salt.

Get the area you're cleaning wet and then use this cleaner to scrub it. Since this cleaner is abrasive, it shouldn't be used as your regular cleaner. Use it on tough jobs and stick to one of the previous two cleaners for the lighter cleaning tasks.

Shower curtains can be difficult to clean because they move around as you're scrubbing them. Take the easy way out by removing shower curtains and tossing them in the washing machine. Air-dry them, as the dryer will melt certain materials.

Hard water deposits can really start to build up on faucets and shower heads. If left to their own accord, they'll eventually start to clog the nozzles the water sprays out of. Faucets and fixtures can be cleaned with a solution of white vinegar and water. Clogged showerheads can be cleared by filling a bag with white vinegar and attaching the bag to the showerhead. Let the showerhead sit in the white vinegar overnight. Rinse and repeat until the nozzles are unclogged.

Mildew and mold can rapidly take hold and start to grow in bathroom that's left damp. One way to prevent this is to air out the bathroom regularly by opening a window and to let natural light into the bathroom by keeping curtains open. Leave fans on while you shower and let them run for 30 minutes after the shower is complete.

To remove mildew and mold and to prevent it from quickly growing back, use this **mold cleaner** to remove the mold:

- 1 cup vinegar.

- 1 cup borax.
- 8 cups water.
- 5 drops tea tree essential oil.

Spray it on the moldy spot and let it sit for a little while before wiping the mold or mildew away. Spray the area with hydrogen peroxide after cleaning it to further kill the mold.

Toilets

Toilets are my least favorite item in the house to clean, for obvious reasons. I wear rubber gloves while cleaning the toilet, but even then I find myself picturing germs crawling their way up the gloves and onto my arms. Every second spent scrubbing the toilet is an agonizing exercise in self-control.

The following **toilet cleaner** can be added to toilets and left there for a couple hours in order to get them clean:

- ½ cup baking soda.
- 1 cup white vinegar.
- ½ cup hydrogen peroxide.

All that usually has to be done after letting this solution sit in the toilet is a quick wipe down with a toilet brush to get the inside of the toilet clean. The same recipe can be used to clean the outside of the toilet. Use a damp sponge and go easy on the cleaner on the outside.

Toilets can harbor urine in tough to reach places. If your bathroom smells like urine and you can't figure out why, you may need to remove the toilet seat and bolt caps and clean all the hard to reach places.

Hard water can cause rings to form in the toilet near the bottom of the bowl. The above recipe should work to eliminate hard water stains, but sometimes you might need a little extra help. A pumice stone can be used to scrape away hard water stains, but it's going to take some elbow grease. Make sure the area you're cleaning is covered with water or you run the risk of scratching the porcelain surface.

Deodorizing the Room

If there was ever a room that needs frequent deodorizing, it's the bathroom. For the longest time, I lived in a house that only had one bathroom shared by 4 people. If you were one of the last people in the bathroom in the morning, it would be all but uninhabitable if it weren't for air freshener. Even then, the spray was barely adequate if you were the 3rd or 4th person in the bathroom.

Making the switch to green cleaning products doesn't mean you have to forgo the air freshener. In fact, you can freshen the air even better than you can when using synthetic scents. Natural air fresheners don't just mask the scent like the synthetic air fresheners do; they completely eliminate it.

The following recipe can be used to make **natural air freshener**:

- 1 cup water.
- ¼ cup white vinegar.
- 10 to 15 drops of essential oil.

The essential oils you use are up to you. You can use a single oil like lavender or lemon or you can blend oils together to create your own unique aromatic blend. For stronger air freshener, you can add 5 to 10 more drops of essential oil to the recipe.

Another method you can use to keep the room smelling good all the time is to purchase a vapor mist diffuser that can be used to disperse essential oils into the room. This will keep your bathroom (or any room, for that matter) smelling fresh as it periodically vaporizes essential oils into a fine mist and disperses them into the room.

Septic Tank

If you live in a house with a septic tank and are like most homeowners, you probably don't give a whole lot of thought to what's going on in the tank. You know the stuff you flush down the toilet and run down the drain makes its way into the tank, but the system is largely out of sight and out of mind.

In the case of septic tanks, what you don't know can really hurt you.

A failed septic tank can release sewage that can then make its way into the groundwater, making everyone who comes in contact with it sick. You may not know you have a leak for years, until the system completely fails and you end up having to replace it at a cost that can run more than $10K for some systems. Depending on the jurisdiction you live in, you may be on the hook for big fines and clean-up costs if a tank you own leaks and pollutes nearby waterways.

Your septic system contains living microorganisms that process everything that makes its way into the tank, so the material you flush and wash down the drain can have an impact on the health of your system. Avoid washing grease and food items down the drain and don't flush anything that isn't human waste down the toilet. Synthetic chemical cleaners, drain cleaners and bleach can all negatively impact the health of your system.

Most natural cleaners are gentle and won't do much harm, if any, to the bacteria in your septic system. Borax, vinegar and baking soda are all less harmful alternatives to the harsh chemicals found in commercial cleaners and will be much easier on your septic tank over time. It's still a good idea to keep use of these cleaners to the bare minimum needed, as some of the cleaners you'll be using are mildly antibacterial.

Living Room

After cleaning the kitchen and the bathroom, the rest of the rooms in the house are going to be a breeze. The living room is one of the easier rooms to stay on top of, as it doesn't have as many areas to gather clutter as the kitchen and bathrooms.

Don't get me wrong, clutter can build up. If you have kids, your living or family room can get cluttered with toys and other objects that need to be picked up daily, lest they turn into a bigger mess. You'll also have to keep an eye out for stray articles of clothing like shoes and coats that get tossed on the floor or the couch.

While the living room is easier than the other rooms we've discussed thus far to clean, it's usually bigger than those rooms, so you have to make sure you don't get sidetracked. It's all too easy to walk into the living room intending to clean and end up watching TV or sitting at the computer instead.

Furniture

Furniture is made of wood, fabric, synthetic material, leather or any combination of the aforementioned materials. You may need multiple cleaners for your furniture, as there isn't a magic formula that's a catch-all for all of these materials.

Natural wood furniture polish can be used to clean and condition some furniture. Mix a cup of jojoba oil with 5 tablespoons of fresh lemon juice and a tablespoon of vinegar. This formula can be used to cover up light scratches. You can also use this **wood cleaner**, which is the same cleaner used to clean wood counters:

- 2 cups warm water.
- 5 tablespoons liquid castile soap.
- 5 drops lemon essential oil.

To clean furniture made from fabric and synthetic fabric, first vacuum up all the loose debris. If there's food or other stains that need to be removed, try blotting them out with a soft cloth dipped in club soda. Deeper set stains may require **fabric stain remover** made of equal parts vinegar and water. Hydrogen peroxide will sometimes pull stains out of lighter materials, but there's a chance of fading.

Leather furniture is durable, but requires special care to keep it in good shape. There are two types of leather used to make furniture: suede and finished leather. Finished leather is easier to take care of than suede, which is much easier to damage. Finished leather can be cleaned with a **leather cleaning solution** made by adding a few tablespoons of liquid castile soap to 2 cups of water. Suede should be kept clean using a damp cloth with nothing added to it. Regardless of the leather type, keep it out of direct sunlight to prevent fading and keep it clear of heat sources because they'll cause it to dry out and crack.

You can clean and revitalize finished leather using **leather conditioner** made from the following ingredients:

- 1 cup linseed oil.
- ½ cup vinegar.

Olive oil or flaxseed oil can be substituted for the linseed oil. Dab a tiny bit of this oil onto a soft cloth and rub it into a wide expanse of leather.

If you can find a tag on your furniture, it may provide you with information as to what types of cleaners are acceptable for that piece of furniture. It's best to call a professional in for the more difficult jobs, as you don't want to have to replace expensive furniture if you ruin it.

Windows and Window Treatments

This section doesn't just apply to the living room. Windows and window treatments are found throughout the house and the techniques laid out in this section can be used on all of your windows, not just the large ones in your living room.

Windows are easy to clean, but it's difficult to keep them looking like they're clean. Use the wrong product and your clean windows will still look dirty because there will be streaks or water spots left on the glass. You can use this **window cleaner** recipe to clean glass and leave it free of streaks and spots:

- 2 teaspoons liquid castile soap.
- ½ cup vinegar.
- 3 cups water.

Clean the windows and wipe them dry with newspaper and you should have glass that's as clear as, well, glass. If streaking is still a problem with this recipe, eliminate the castile soap and try adding a tablespoon of lemon juice instead.

Window screens can be cleaned with **window screen cleaner** made by combining the following ingredients:

- ¼ cup baking soda.
- 4 cups water.
- 5 drops tea tree essential oil.

Spray the cleaner on the screen and let it sit for a few minutes before wiping the screen down. You might have to take really dirty screens down and hose them off before this cleaner will work effectively.

There are a number of window treatments you may have to clean. Here are some tips as to how to clean various window treatments:

- **Wood.** Wood shutters or blinds should be dusted regularly. Wipe them down with a damp cloth a few times a year. Don't use anything more than water on wood shutters or blinds.
- **Fabric.** Fabric drapes and curtains can be vacuumed using the drapery attachment on a vacuum cleaner. Some materials are machine-washable and can be laundered at home. Other materials have to be taken to the dry cleaners for cleaning.
- **Solar shades.** Solar shades should be dusted regularly. They can be spot-cleaned using a mixture of 2 cups of water and a tablespoon of liquid castile soap.
- **Pleated.** Pleated shades can be dusted. This is the only cleaning you can do with this type of shade, so stay on top of it to make sure they don't get too dirty.
- **Metal or plastic blinds.** Metal and synthetic blinds should be dusted regularly. Use a damp rag to clean the blinds using this recipe. Vinyl blinds can be taken down and brought to the shower or tub to be rinsed off.
- **Mini blinds.** Mini blinds can be taken down and brought outside to be hosed off.

Cleaning blinds is a time consuming task no matter how you look at it. To speed things up, place old socks over your hands and get the socks damp with the cleaning recipe you're using. You'll have more control over where the socks go than you would if you were holding a rag and will be able to make short work of the blinds.

You may find the window sills or the frames of your windows have mold or mildew growing on or in them. Mold and mildew can be removed using this **natural mold remover**:

- 2 tablespoons washing soda.
- 1 quart water.
- ½ cup 3% hydrogen peroxide.

Combine the washing soda and water and use it to clean up the mold or mildew. Spray the area with 3% hydrogen peroxide to ensure mold and mildew doesn't come back.

TVs and Monitors

Over time, the screens on your TVs, computers and laptops can accumulate a lot of dust. Weekly dustings with a microfiber cloth will get rid of most of the dust, but you'll occasionally need to wipe the screens down with a damp rag.

You could run out and buy expensive screen cleaners, but there's really no need to. Screen cleaner that's safe for most screens, including LCD and plasma monitors can be made by mixing equal parts vinegar and distilled water. Spray a microfiber cloth with the cleaner and wipe the monitor clean using the cloth. Don't spray the cleaner directly on the monitor.

Whatever you do, don't use paper towels to clean your screens. They'll scratch your monitor and the damage can accumulate over time. Don't use tap water for this recipe. The minerals in tap water can also build up over time and create an opaque sheen on your screen.

If you have scratches on your screen, you may be able to get rid of the scratch using petroleum jelly. Dab it onto the scratch with a cotton ball and wipe the jelly away with a microfiber cloth. Minor scratches will all but disappear using this trick.

Fireplace

Wood burning fireplaces are advantageous in that they allow you to save money on heating costs by burning wood instead of using gas and electricity to warm your home. They do require maintenance and failure to maintain your fireplace can have dire consequences. Every year you hear about houses that burn down due to fires that started in the chimney or around the fireplace.

Chimney cleaning is one of the few areas of the house I don't recommend cleaning yourself. A professional inspection and yearly cleaning will give you peace of mind and will help ensure your fireplace is in good working order. Monitor your fireplace closely for creosote buildup, which is a black substance that builds up on the walls of the fireplace and chimney, and soot and get the fireplace cleaned if you notice they're starting to build up. Both creosote and soot are flammable and can cause fires if allowed to grow unchecked.

Ashes will need to be cleaned out regularly. Wear a mask when you clean them out. They can be swept out or vacuumed up.

In addition to cleaning the inside of the fireplace, the hearth will also need to be cleaned regularly. A vacuum cleaner with a duster attachment can be used to remove dust and soot from the hearth. The following **stone fireplace hearth cleaner** can be used to clean most stone hearths:

- 1 cup liquid castile soap.
- 5 tablespoons salt.

- 2 quarts warm water.

Let the cleaner sit for 15 minutes after applying it. Wear gloves and scrub the hearth with a rag or a sponge. A plastic scrub brush can be used to clean particularly dirty areas of the hearth.

Brick fireplace cleaner uses a different recipe. Here are the ingredients used to naturally clean a brick fireplace:

- 1 cup washing soda.
- 4 cups warm water.
- ½ cup castile soap.
- ½ cup salt.

Apply the cleaner and let it soak in for 15 minutes before scrubbing it away with a plastic scrub brush. White vinegar can also be used to remove stuck-on soot and creosote.

Bedrooms

The bedrooms are probably going to be the easiest rooms in the house to clean. That is, unless you have kids like mine, who put off cleaning until their bedrooms are on the verge of becoming a Superfund site. Then it can be a monumental task just getting rid of the clutter.

Bedroom furniture can be cleaned using the same furniture cleaners and spot removers used in the living room. Dust the fronts and tops of dressers regularly with an electrostatic duster and polish them with the wood polish from the Living Room Furniture section.

Bedding

Bedding is one of the most ignored items in most households. Sheets, blankets, quilts and pillowcases are often ignored for months, while drool, dead skin, bodily fluids and all sorts of other contaminants build up on them. Regular cleaning of your bedding is essential to staying healthy, as you spend much of your time in bed.

Regular laundering of your bedding will keep it clean and will potentially keep you healthier as a result. When you consider you probably spend more time in your bed each week than you do on any other piece of furniture in your house, the importance of cleaning bedding becomes apparent.

Powdered castile laundry soap works well on bedding. Here's the recipe for the soap:

- 4 cups borax.
- 4 cups washing soda.
- 2 cups finely-grated castile bar soap.
- 4 tablespoons baking soda.

If you have a smaller washing machine, you may not be able to wash bedding in it. If that's the case, a trip to the Laundromat may be in order.

Mattresses

Even though they're covered by sheets and mattress covers, mattresses still need regular cleaning. It's a good idea to clean your mattress every time you change your sheets. Dust particles, skin oils and bodily fluids can all make their way down into your mattress.

The first things you should do to keep your mattress clean is to vacuum it regularly. This will remove dirt and dust particles that will stain your mattress if moisture makes its way down to the mattress.

Check the mattress for stains and clean them up using the following **mattress cleaner recipe**:

- 3 tablespoons castile soap.
- 2 cups warm water.
- 2 tablespoons fresh lemon juice.

Apply the cleaner to the mattress and let it soak in for 10 minutes. Blot up as much of the cleaner as you can. Repeat the process until the stain is gone.

This cleaner lifts most stains, with blood stains being the most obvious exception. To remove bloodstains from a mattress, apply hydrogen peroxide directly to the mattress and blot it up as it bubbles. Once it stops bubbling wash as much of the hydrogen peroxide out of the fabric as you can using the mattress cleaner we just talked about.

Over time, mattresses absorb odors and can become a giant source of stink in your bedroom. To revitalize a musty mattress or one that smells like cigarette smoke, use the following **mattress freshening spray**:

- 2 cups water.
- ½ cup baking soda.
- 10 to 20 drops of your favorite essential oil.

Combine all of the ingredients in a spray bottle and set it to fine mist. Spray the entire mattress and let it dry before putting the bedding back down. This spray can also be used to remove bad smells from bedding, but shouldn't be used in lieu of regular washing.

Laundry Room

The laundry room is a place where you do a lot of cleaning, but the laundry room itself needs periodic cleaning from time to time as well. The soaps and cleaners you use in the laundry room can build up in your appliances over time and reduce their effectiveness.

Sinks, cabinets and floors can be cleaned using the recipes from previous sections of this chapter.

Washers and Dryers

While it may seem counterintuitive, washing machines and dryers need periodic cleaning. Soap scum, grease and lint can all build up in your washer and dryer to reduce effectiveness. Failure to keep your washer and dryer clean can drastically shorten their lifespan, costing you a lot of money in the long run.

Clean top-loading washing machines by letting the machine fill with hot water and then adding a quart of white vinegar to the machine. Let it agitate for a few minutes and then turn the machine off and let the water and vinegar sit. While it's sitting, use a soft cloth and Q-tips to clean all of the nooks and crannies of the machine.

To clean front-loaders, fill the machine with hot water on the "clean cycle" and add 2 to 3 cups of white vinegar to the machine. Let the machine run through the complete wash cycle. Once the wash cycle is complete, open the door and use a soft cloth and Q-tips to clean all the hard to reach areas.

Don't forget the fabric softener and detergent dispensers when you clean your machines. They can usually be removed. Clean them with white vinegar as well.

White vinegar can also be used to clean the inside of your dryer, but you're going to have to do it manually. This means a lot more scrubbing. Don't leave the dryer soaking wet. Dry it out when you're done. Don't forget the lint trap. You need to clean lint from the lint trap regularly to keep your dryer in good working order.

Laundry

Store shelves are full of laundry detergents claiming to be "green" or "eco-friendly." Due to the fact that these claims aren't regulated, many of these cleaners contain substances that barely qualify as natural and some are downright dangerous. You're much better off making your own laundry detergent at home.

The following powdered laundry detergent has served me well for many years:

- 4 cups borax.
- 4 cups washing soda.
- 2 cups finely-grated castile bar soap.
- 4 tablespoons baking soda.

Use ¼ cup of this detergent for each load.

If you prefer liquid detergent, try this liquid laundry detergent:

- 2 cups borax.
- 1 cup vinegar.
- 1 cup washing soda.
- ½ cup liquid castile soap.
- 4 cups water.

Use ¾ to 1 cup of this detergent per load of laundry.

Here's a natural alternative to laundry soap that most people have never heard of: soap nuts. **Soap nuts** are berries that produce a natural soap called **saponin** when added to water. Add several soap nuts to a load of laundry and the soap nut will create all the natural soap you need to get your clothes clean.

If you have clothes that need softening or have yellow stains on them, add half a cup of white vinegar to the load during the rinse cycle. Vinegar softens fabric while preventing yellowing. Lemon juice can also be added during the rinse cycle to brighten white clothing.

Don't forget the **color catchers**. These handy little sheets of fabric will catch dye that's floating around the washing machine before it makes its way into other articles of clothing. They lengthen the useful life of your clothing by protecting them from sucking up die from the rest of your clothes. If you've ever washed whites with darker colors and had your whites take on a different hue, you've seen the effects of die floating around the washer.

Here's the recipe for color catchers:

- 3 tablespoons washing soda.
- 2 cups warm water.
- Cotton fabric.

Combine the washing soda and warm water and dip the cotton fabric into it. Let the fabric dry and cut it into squares. Toss a square in with your laundry and you'll eliminate much of the worry of having colors bleed into your lighter clothes. I still wouldn't wash dark clothes with white clothes, but the rest of your colored clothes will be safer.

Dryer sheets can be eliminated by purchasing wool balls that can be thrown in with your laundry. Throwing 5 of these balls into the dryer with your wet laundry will reduce static and make your clothes dry faster.

Keeping the House Clean

I know there are some people reading this book who are having trouble keeping the house clean. One of the biggest complaints I hear when it comes to green cleaning is people who say they don't have time to clean house using normal products, let alone green products. They think adding green products to their already stressful cleaning regime would be too much.

If you're one of those people, this chapter's for you. Using green products doesn't make cleaning any harder. In fact, it can make cleaning easier, as you'll only have to have a handful of items on hand that you can mix to make whatever cleaner it is you need at the time. Most recipes can be premixed, or they can be mixed as you need them, whichever is more convenient.

To be completely honest with you, most of my cleaning these days is done with a simple solution of water and vinegar with a bit of lemon essential oil added to mix. If this cleaner doesn't get the job done, then I turn to the big guns, but most messes are easy to clean up as long as you jump on them right away.

As far as finding time to clean goes, you have to make time.

If you're anything like the average person these days, you lead a busy life and have trouble finding time to clean house. It's all too easy to start cleaning and then get sidetracked by a phone call, younger family members in need of assistance, the Internet, TV or any number of other distractions life decides to throw your way. Creating a master cleaning plan that includes a schedule will allow you to stick to the plan and get your house clean.

The first step is always the toughest. In order to make housecleaning manageable, you're going to have to give your entire house a good deep cleaning. A deep cleaning from top to bottom won't be easy, but it'll set the stage for the easier to manage step of maintaining an already clean house. When you let things go for even a short period of time, dirt, dust and clutter can really start to build up. It seems like no sooner do you focus your efforts on one area of the house than another is starting to slip out of control.

When this happens, it's usually because things have devolved to the point where the entire house needs deep cleaning. Instead of simply maintaining an already clean house, deep cleaning is required each and every time you clean a room. Deep cleaning takes a lot more time than maintaining, so you end up spending more time cleaning than you would if you started with a relatively clean house.

The ultimate goal is to get to the maintaining stage and stay there.

The best way to do this is to focus on one room at a time and clean that room from top to bottom. Break the cleaning jobs in the room into individual tasks and focus on each task until it's done. Once you start a task, don't let anything short of a major emergency stop you before it's done. It's going to be tough at first because you're used to allowing yourself to get distracted, but you'll soon become a cleaning machine.

Before you start cleaning a room, sit down and create a checklist that lays out all of the cleaning tasks that need to be done in the room. Break them into individual tasks that can be completed in a single session. As you go through the room and complete cleaning tasks one at a time, you'll be able to cross them off the list. This will do a couple things for you. It'll keep you motivated because you'll be able to see the progress you're making and it'll help you build momentum as you work toward your ultimate goal of a clean house.

What I'm about to tell you next is key to keeping your house clean. Once you've cleaned an area of the house, keep it that way. This is the only way you're going to be able to keep up.

If you've removed clutter from the flat surfaces of a room and scrubbed them clean, it's easy to make a quick pass through that room at the end of each day to make sure there are no new items resting on the flat surfaces. It's also easy to wipe them down real quick. Wait a week or two and you'll likely end up with a cluttered mess that's much more difficult to clean. You'll have to clear all the clutter and then clean the hidden messes and stains you find beneath the clutter. A simple 15 minutes cleaning job can quickly become an arduous task that takes hours if you don't keep on top of the cleaning.

Here's a quick summary of what needs to be done:

1. **Break the house up into rooms.**
2. **Identify all of the deep cleaning tasks in the room that need to be done.** Break them up into manageable chunks and create a checklist.

3. **Get to work.** Cross each item off the list as it's completed. This step can take a significant amount of time if your house is dirty. If you've got a good support group, you may be able to enlist the help of friends and family members. If not, you may want to hire a maid service to help you get back on track.
4. **Once you've completed an area, maintain that area by ensuring it stays clean.**

No matter what you do, there will always be items that need maintenance or deep cleaning. Keep a list of these items and designate a few weekends a year to work on the deep cleaning and maintenance tasks that need to be done. The rest of your time should be spent maintaining the already clean house.

Here's another bit of advice that came straight from a friend in the hotel service industry. Start at the top of the room and work your way down. Clean the dust off of the tops of cabinets and ceiling fans first. Work your way down to lower areas of the room. Clean higher cabinets first, then countertops, then the cabinets below countertops. Continue until you get to the floor and clean the floor last. This saves you time because as you clean the higher areas, dust and grime will fall onto everything below the item you're cleaning. If you clean the floor first, it's going to be dirty again by the time you're done cleaning other areas of the room.

Stick with it. It's a lot harder to clean a house in fits and spurts than it is to keep it clean. You can be your own best friend or your worst enemy in this regard.

Appendix: Recipe Quick Reference Guide

Air Freshener:

1 cup vinegar.

10 to 20 drops of essential oil (lemon, orange and lavender are popular choices).

1 cup water.

All-Purpose Cleaner #1:

1 tablespoon borax.

1 cup water.

All-Purpose Cleaner #2:

½ cup baking soda.

½ cup borax.

5 tablespoons vinegar.

1 cup liquid castile soap.

10 to 20 drops of essential oils (Lemon, lavender and tea tree oil are all good choices.

4 cups water.

All-Purpose Cleaner #3:

1 cup vinegar.

2 cups water.

All-Purpose Kitchen Cleaner:

1 quart warm water.

5 tablespoons baking soda.

5 tablespoons liquid castile soap.

Ant Killer:

1 cup borax.

1 cup granulated sugar.

Antibacterial Cleaner:

2 cups warm water.

½ cup castile soap.

¼ cup baking soda.

10 drops lavender essential oil.

10 drops tea tree essential oil.

Antibacterial Hand Soap:

3 tablespoons liquid castile soap.

1 cup distilled water.

1 teaspoon vitamin E oil.

5 drops lavender essential oil.

3 drops tea tree essential oil.

Brass and Copper Cleaner:

2 tablespoons salt.

½ cup vinegar.

½ cup lemon juice.

Brick Fireplace Cleaner:

1 cup washing soda.

4 cups warm water.

½ cup castile soap.

½ cup salt.

Bug Spray:

1 cup borax.

1 cup granulated sugar.

1 quart water.

Cabinet Cleaner:

1 quart warm water.

1 tablespoon baking soda.

2 teaspoons liquid castile soap.

2 tablespoons vinegar.

OPTIONAL: 5 drops lemon essential oil.

Carpet Cleaner:

½ cup baking soda.

1 cup white vinegar.

1 cup borax.

Carpet Stain Remover #1:

1 cup vinegar.

4 tablespoons salt.

3 tablespoons borax.

Carpet Stain Remover #2:

1 cup club soda.

1 cup cornstarch.

Coffee Maker Cleaner:

1 cup vinegar.

4 cups hot water.

Coffee Pot Cleaner:

2 tablespoons salt.

2 cups water.

Color Catchers:

3 tablespoons washing soda.

2 cups warm water.

Cotton fabric.

Concrete Counter Cleaner:

2 tablespoons liquid castile soap.

2 cups water.

Concrete Stain Removal Paste:

3 tablespoons hydrogen peroxide.

1 cup flour.

½ cup water.

Cutting Board Cleaner:

½ cup baking soda.

1 lemon.

Degreaser:

½ cup fresh lemon juice.

¼ cup castile soap.

1 cup water.

Denture Cleaner:

2 tablespoons baking soda.

1 cup water.

Dish Detergent # 1 (Powder):

½ cup citric acid.

½ cup washing soda.

¼ cup baking soda.

5 tablespoons sea salt.

Dish Detergent # 2 (Powder):

1 cup borax.

1 cup baking soda.

Dish Detergent #3 (Liquid):

½ cup liquid castile soap.

2 cups water.

1 cup white vinegar.

2 tablespoons washing soda.

2 tablespoons fresh lemon juice.

3 tablespoons salt.

10 drops lemon or tea tree essential oil.

Dish Soap (Liquid):

2 cups liquid castile soap.

5 tablespoons water.

5 to 10 drops antibacterial essential oil (lemon or tea tree oil work well).

Disinfectant Spray:

2 cups vinegar.

2 cups 3% hydrogen peroxide.

Drain Cleaner #1:

1 cup borax.

2 cups boiling water.

Dry Shampoo:

2 cups baking soda.

1 cup cornstarch.

2 tablespoons ground cloves.

Fabric Furniture Stain Remover:

½ cup white vinegar.

½ cup water.

Fizzy Cleaners:

1 ½ cups baking soda.

½ cup citric acid.

20 drops lemon essential oil.

15 drops peppermint essential oil.

Water.

Floor Cleaner #1:

1 cup baking soda.

1 gallon warm water.

Floor Cleaner #2:

2 tablespoons liquid castile soap.

1 gallon water.

Flower Preserver:

1 part borax.

2 parts cornmeal or oatmeal.

Foaming Drain Cleaner:

1 cup vinegar.

1 cup baking soda

1 cup table salt.

2 cups boiling water.

Fridge Cleaner:

1 quart warm water.

10 tablespoons baking soda or washing soda.

5 tablespoons liquid castile soap.

Fruit and Vegetable Rinse:

½ cup hydrogen peroxide.

½ cup water.

Granite Cleaner:

2 tablespoons liquid castile soap.

1 cup water.

OPTIONAL: 1 cup baking soda.

OPTIONAL: 2 tablespoons hydrogen peroxide.

Grill and Battery Terminal Cleaner:

5 tablespoons water.

1 cup baking soda.

Grill Cleaner #2:

1 cup hydrogen peroxide.

2 cups baking soda.

Grout Cleaner #1:

½ cup baking soda.

3 tablespoons of water.

½ cup hydrogen peroxide.

Grout Cleaner #2:

½ cup vinegar.

½ cup baking soda.

½ cup salt.

Grout Cleaning Paste:

2 cups baking soda.

1 cup water.

Grout Mold Cleaning Paste:

3 cups baking soda.

1 cup hydrogen peroxide.

Grout Sealer:

¼ cup beeswax.

1 cup linseed oil.

Laminate Counter Cleaner:

1 cup water.

1 cup vinegar.

3 to 5 drops lemon, tea tree or lavender essential oil.

Laminate Floor Cleaner:

2 cups water.

2 cups white vinegar.

¼ cup castile soap.

5 to 10 drops of lavender and tea tree essential oils.

Laminate Stain Remover:

1 cup baking soda.

½ cup fresh lemon juice.

Laundry Soap (Powdered):

4 cups borax.

4 cups washing soda.

2 cups finely-grated castile bar soap.

4 tablespoons baking soda.

Laundry Soap (Liquid):

2 cups borax.

1 cup vinegar.

1 cup washing soda.

½ cup liquid castile soap.

8 cups water.

Leather Furniture Cleaner:

3 tablespoons liquid castile soap.

2 cups water.

Leather Revitalizer:

½ cup vinegar.

1 cup linseed oil.

Linoleum Floor Cleaner:

1 cup of vinegar.

1 quart water.

OPTIONAL: ½ cup baking soda.

OPTIONAL: 10 to 15 drops lemon or tea tree essential oil.

Linoleum Stain Remover:

½ cup baking soda.

½ cup water.

Marble Cleaner #1:

½ cup baking soda.

½ cup water.

Marble Cleaner #2:

1 tablespoon castile soap.

1 quart warm water.

Mattress Cleaner:

3 tablespoons castile soap.

2 cups warm water.

2 tablespoons fresh lemon juice.

Mattress Freshening Spray:

2 cups water.

½ cup baking soda.

10 to 20 drops of your favorite essential oil.

Metal Polish:

½ cup salt.

½ cup vinegar.

½ cup white flour.

Microwave Cleaner:

½ cup baking soda.

2 cups warm water.

Mineral Deposit Remover:

½ cup vinegar.

1 cup water.

3 tablespoons baking soda.

Mold Cleaner:

1 cup vinegar.

1 cup borax.

8 cups water.

5 drops tea tree essential oil.

Mold Remover:

2 tablespoons washing soda.

1 quart water.

½ cup 3% hydrogen peroxide.

Monitor Cleaner:

½ cup vinegar.

½ cup distilled water.

Oven Cleaner:

½ cup washing soda.

1 cup liquid castile soap.

5 to 10 drops eucalyptus essential oil.

Oven Spill Cleaner:

½ cup salt.

1 tablespoon cinnamon.

Pot and Pan Cleaner:

½ cup cooking oil.

¼ cup sea salt.

Room Deodorizer:

½ cup baking soda.

½ cup fresh lemon juice.

Rust Remover #1:

1 cup borax.

2 cups warm water.

2 tablespoons lemon juice.

Rust Remover #2:

1 cup salt.

¼ cup cream of tartar.

Water.

Shampoo:

1 tablespoon liquid castile soap.

4 tablespoons water.

Scouring Paste:

½ cup borax.

½ cup baking soda.

2 cups hot water.

Silver Polish:

½ cup baking soda.

6 tablespoons salt.

8 cups water.

Silver Tarnish Remover:

5 tablespoons salt.

5 tablespoons baking soda.

4 cups water.

Aluminum foil.

Sink Stain Remover:

2 cups borax.

½ cup lemon juice.

4 drops eucalyptus essential oil.

Splinter Remover:

½ cup baking soda.

1 cup water.

Stain Remover #1:

1 cup borax.

2 cups water.

Stain Remover #2:

¼ cup washing soda.

½ cup water.

¼ cup hydrogen peroxide.

Sticky Residue Remover:

1 cup coconut oil.

1 cup baking soda.

5 drops lemon essential oil.

Stone Hearth Fireplace Cleaner:

1 cup liquid castile soap.

5 tablespoons salt.

2 quarts warm water.

Stovetop Cleaner:

1 cup washing soda.

¼ cup salt.

1 cup hot water.

Tile Cleaner:

1 cup vinegar.

2 cups water.

Toilet Cleaner:

½ cup baking soda.

1 cup white vinegar.

OPTIONAL: ½ cup hydrogen peroxide.

Towel Cleaner:

¾ cup baking soda.

1 cup white vinegar.

Toy Cleaner:

2 tablespoons baking soda.

2 cups water.

Tub and Tile Cleaner #1:

1 cup liquid castile soap.

3 cups water.

1 cup baking soda.

Tub and Tile Cleaner #2:

1 cup vinegar.

1 cup water.

10 drops lemon essential oil.

Tub and Shower Cleaner (Abrasive):

½ cup baking soda.

½ cup borax.

½ cup salt.

Vinyl Floor Cleaner:

1 cup apple cider vinegar.

2 quarts water.

Vinyl Floor Stain Remover:

½ cup baking soda.

½ cup white vinegar.

Whitening Toothpaste:

½ cup hydrogen peroxide.

1 cup baking soda.

½ cup warm water.

A few drops of peppermint essential oil.

Window Cleaner:

2 teaspoons liquid castile soap.

½ cup vinegar.

3 cups water.

Window Screen Cleaner:

¼ cup baking soda.

4 cups water.

5 drops tea tree essential oil.

Wood Counter Cleaner

2 cups warm water.

5 tablespoons liquid castile soap.

5 drops lemon essential oil.

Wood Floor Cleaner:

Half a cup of vinegar

A gallon of water.

¼ cup castile soap.

Wood Floor Polish:

¼ cup vegetable oil (I prefer olive oil).

3 tablespoons vinegar.

2 tablespoons vodka.

OPTIONAL: 2 to 3 tablespoons fresh lemon juice.

Wood Floor Polish #2:

4 cups green tea.

5 to 10 drops lemon essential oil.

Wood Floor Water Mark Remover:

1 cup jojoba oil.

5 to 10 drops lemon or orange essential oil.

Wood Floor Wax:

½ cup almond oil.

½ cup vodka.

3 tablespoons palm wax.

3 tablespoons bees wax, grated.

Wood Furniture Polish:

1 cup jojoba oil.

5 tablespoons fresh lemon juice.

1 tablespoon vinegar.

Wood Polish:

3 tablespoons sea salt.

1 cup olive oil.

½ cup white vinegar.

Wood Revitalizer:

3 tablespoons vinegar.

1 tablespoon jojoba oil.

10 drops lemon essential oil.

Wood Scratch Remover:

1 cup vinegar.

Iodine.

Printed in Great Britain
by Amazon.co.uk, Ltd.,
Marston Gate.